Lind

Strange V......

velvet

LINDA'S STRANGE VACATION
Marcus Huttning
ISBN 1 871592 83 6
A Velvet Book
Copyright © Velvet Publications 1997
All rights reserved
Published by
VELVET PUBLICATIONS
83 Clerkenwell Road
London EC1, UK
Tel: 0171-430-9878
Fax: 0171-242-5527
A Bondagebest Production

Design:
Bradley Davis, PCP International

chapter one

Linda arrived at her uncle's villa. A splendid sun paved a golden pathway to the white stucco mansion gleaming like a clean sheet under a soft blue sky. The young girl's eyes sparkled in the yellow day that poured its transparent veil of gold over the rocks, the joyful pines and the dappled sea. One week of vacation, one long relaxful week, had just begun.

"Here we are." Lola waved. She met the youngster at the station in her small sports car.

Linda had not met the blonde woman before, and she was not at all surprised. Her uncle Arthur changed his mistresses often, and this did not go without notice in the family. Despite their attempt at hiding their shock at his behaviour, it managed to blurt out at the most unexpected moments. The family was composed of uncles and aunts. Their parents were dead, but an inheritance saw them through the more troubling aspects of their material existence. Even Linda was fortunate in being protected by a small annuity which not only gave her a college education, which she was now undergoing in a girl's school near London, but also offered her independence and a certain ease of mind. She had been receiving the consoling sum of some £125 since the age of ten. It was enough to permit her to expand her wings and yawn without a true worry in the world. If she needed more, there was always uncle Arthur and the others.

"Oh, I like this auto." These were her first words opening the conversation which had to begin at one time or another. She smiled at Lola in an effort to win the woman's friendship.

Lola was the first to climb out of the late model two-seater. She moved with alacrity and pride. She was only wearing a pair of shorts, cut extremely high and showing a lovely pair of bronzed legs, long and shapely. A mere blouse which had been negligently buttoned could not hide her luscious solid breasts, almost popping out of her opened sporty chemise.

Instinctively Linda compared her own 'quality' with that of her companion, whom she estimated to be about twenty-five years old. She had been complimented on her beauty many times, although there were those horrible low whistles she loathed in the streets of London. After all, they were compliments in a way. Feeling appreciated by all, the significant and the insignificant, was a source of well-being and assurance for the young girl. Naively and a little fearful, she wondered whether she would not appear too thin in contrast to her uncle's favourite, especially when she put on a bathing suit. The idea was quickly dropped as Lola signalled her to follow. Valise in hand, she stumbled after Lola toward the house.

"You'll like it here. You'll see." The young woman opened the door and continued to praise the merits of the locale. "There isn't a house around for miles. The beach on rocks are so deserted that you can go in bathing completely nude."

Linda's eyes slipped to the floor on the last hanging words of the sentence. She felt that Lola had brought them out as a jibe, but then she pinched herself for groping with her hypersensitive imagination.

She smiled back timidly. Her eyes caught the steel glance of the handsome woman. Linda was able to visualize Lola's superb body perfectly modelling the deserted beach with its bronze-golden tint.

Her mental picture was diluted when a boy rushed out of the house without a word or gesture. He was clothed in scanty bathing trunks and a towel thrown over his left shoulder. His aspect was young, perhaps he was fifteen or so, and his body had a feline grace that was exhibited in his slightest movement.

Lola called to him and asked him to come back for a moment.

"Here is your cousin Robert, Linda. Come here, Robert, and say hello to your cousin."

Linda had only seen Robert once in her life. She was about nine at the time and he was five or six. Their infantile capers did not register in their memories. Robert was the only child of one of Linda's sisters, a half-sister on the part of her mother who had been married and divorced four or five times. Uncle Arthur was a brother of her mother, and, in a way, a chip of the old block.

She barely remembered the young lad.

"Hi there," Robert said approaching his newly discovered cousin. Linda noticed that the boy had a peculiar ironic smile which curled his lower lip. His eyes switched from her to Lola and then he looked her up and down as though he were measuring her for a beauty contest.

"Did you have a good trip?"

It was hard to know just how to take him, so Linda responded as politely as she could. There was no sense making enemies over a simple question, however tainted it may have seemed.

"Oh, yes, thank you. This is a magnificent place. I think I shall like it here."

"You'll see that it is even better than you might imagine." He literally twitched with irony and his smile broadened.

"Why don't you come for a swim?" he proposed affably.

Lola interjected with her right as an adult seeing things in their proper proportion.

"No, wait awhile. Linda has only just arrived. We'll see you later. Is Arthur in the library?"

"Gee, I don't know. The last time I was in there I didn't see him."

Lola took Linda's hand and led her away from the chipper, ironic puppy. Robert had a tendency to be a little heavy in his humour and Lola walked out or turned her back when she sensed he was on the verge of playing the wise-guy.

"Come along," Lola said with a wholesome winning smile. "I'll show you your room."

Once alone, Linda arranged her belongings neatly, and every now and then she looked out of the half-opened window. The view was magnificent. There was a scent in the air that she rediscovered. It had been three years since she inhaled that marvellous perfume of the sea and pines combined. The woods buzzed with the sound of a million happy insects.

She laid her swimming suit out on the armchair by the window. It was a small two-piece affair, brightly coloured. From her suitcase she took her toilet articles and placed them on the glass ledge in front of the mirror.

Linda thought of the quaint villa and of the few rooms she had seen. It was curious to see the first-floor lined with bedrooms and she immediately thought of the Walpole Inn she had stayed at during Christmas time. She still hadn't seen the library, the kitchen or the maid's room.

Suddenly someone knocked on the door, and opened it without waiting for a response. It was Lola.

"Are you ready?" she asked. The bronzed-skin women was wearing a green beach-robe which was slightly wrapped at the waist by a simple cord. Linda saw Lola's splendid muscular legs and noticed that she was wearing a tiny bikini that barely hid her pubic hair. The upper part resembled a thin mask and failed to conceal the round ample breasts. The points of her nipples stood brazenly firm in the small pockets of the meagre bra.

"I'll be ready in a jiffy," Linda reassured Lola.

"Good. Don't rush, we have time." As she smoked, Lola stretched out on the bed and brought out a pack of cigarettes from her robe pocket as well as a gold-plated lighter. She lit her cigarette and inhaled deeply.

"Oh, excuse me. You don't smoke, do you?" Lola had forgotten that she was with an adolescent adult.

"No, I don't smoke. Well, that is, I smoke in college once in a blue moon. You know how it is?"

Linda began to get undressed slowly. She was rather shy and not used to having another person in the same room when she stripped down. Even at school, where she had a private room, she locked the doors when she undressed.

It was true, however, that recently at school a sense of intimacy had grown between her and her mates, and she took more liberties than she had ever done before. Linda didn't want to give the impression of being a recluse. She decided to undress as though she had been doing it all her life in front of friends. Lola was a friend, or at least, she hoped she was going to be one.

All in all, Linda was intimidated. She might not have been, but the continual look that Lola gave her troubled her. The eyes of the lounging woman scrutinized her and they were filled with a glint of curiosity and mystery.

Just when Linda got down to her panties and bra, Lola leaned on her elbow and whispered.

"You're remarkably well-built for your age. You're just sixteen, aren't you?"

Linda, without answering back, turned her head away timidly. It was a gesture in the vague hope that not seeing, would mean not being seen. A stupid illusion of course. But those eyes haunted her and she didn't know quite what to make of them.

She deliberately turned her back to hide her sex as she slid off her undies. Little did she guess that Lola had a perfect view of her tufty triangle, that mass of curly hair that shielded her vulva, by taking advantage of the mirror over the dressing cabinet. Linda, feeling quite protected, slipped off her bra and revealed two remarkable young breasts. They were vibrant and alive with their two rose buttons standing cutely up in the warm summer air. The young girl reached for her bathing suit, still avoiding the glance of the intruder who she was sure was scoping her intently.

She had just placed her hand on her bathing suit when a hand touched her shoulder. It rolled down her back trembling and the touch electrified her.

"What's wrong, Lola?" she asked in a troubled shrill voice with her heart beating quickly.

"Nothing. Nothing at all." Lola's voice was low and hoarse.

She placed her arm around Linda's thin waist and brought her to the bed. The young girl was forced to give into the strange cajoling. Suddenly she found herself stretched on the bed besides the perfumed Lola.

The suddenness of this outrageous action, if that was what she could call it (it may have been a playful act and she would be sorry to be so prudish), caught Linda by surprise and knocked the wind out of her.

She was flat on her lovely back gazing into the large warm eyes of the brown-skinned hostess. Lola's hand wandered over the quivering torso and her fingers played with the belly button and skimmed down to the fuzzy bush that Linda had deemed as sacred territory.

Seeing that the young lass was paralysed with apprehension and fear, Lola placed the same hand, that roving tinkling hand, on the girl's burning cheek. Linda was momentarily released from her sudden scare.

But Lola had not finished fumbling with the intricate and

substantial sectors of the young girl's torso.

Her hand cupped a breast and her long painted fingernails tickled a nipple.

"We ought to be good friends, don't you think so?" she said softly in the same low voice that had begun the interlude.

She lowered her face toward Linda's. The girl remained petrified, but managed to close her eyes in escape. A pair of mature lips brushed the side of her mouth and then found the ample, dry, trembling heart-shaped mouth. A warm tongue, sleek and humid, tried to invade the adolescent's oral reaches. But Linda clenched her teeth, and Lola's impetuous tongue had to meet the obstacle of lovely white enamel.

But Linda could no longer resist the strange sensation that afflicted her all at once. Her mouth opened and her warm breath was met by a seeking tongue which explored the interior of her fresh-rose mouth. The hapless girl felt a hand crawl down her back and grip one of her buttocks. Long fingers encircled her vagina and frictioned the entrance. Linda sighed and the sound astonished her. It had been a long time since she had experienced this odd sensual flame rise in her body. She was troubled, afraid, but happy. It would be impossible for her to resist this voracious woman, who was taking possession of her as one captivates and tames a young animal.

It took her a couple of seconds to realize that she was alone on the bed. Lola had sprung up, brusquely interrupting her caresses. Linda felt neglected. Perhaps another time... but she was being silly and loathsome. Lola extended her arms and it was obvious that she had forgotten everything. She handed Linda her bikini.

"Come. Let's go. The sea is awaiting us." Walking side by side, Linda couldn't help thinking of what had just transpired a few seconds ago in her bedroom. The young girl had never had any sexual rapport. She was a virgin for man and woman. It was true that one night at college, a friend of hers playfully scrambled into her bed, and after some brief words interjected by guffaws and smiles and raw jokes, the friend began a series of caresses that went a little bit further than those of Lola's, but Linda had forgotten about it. Besides, her friend had not made any real impression on her and she tired easily of the slobbering kisses and inept handling of her

---

Linda's Strange Vacation

lower body. Of course, she never was really sure whether that was just a tickling game in fun or the beginning of a rude adventure. Anyway, it had nothing to do with Lola. Lola was different, and horribly dominating, and at the same time terribly attractive.

A swift shiver stimulated Linda's slender backbone.

"It's over there where we usually bathe." Lola pointed to an obscure hidden cove. Linda felt her long handsome fingers once more on her shoulders, only this time they were not insisting, unfortunately.

The sea licked the red rocks with her white frothy tongue. The cove appeared deserted just as Lola described it. Linda was unable to resist the temptation of cooling her toes in the ocean. She threw down her large beach towel and ran to the brim of the water. Lola disrobed herself of her cumbersome apparel and followed the lithe, graceful girl.

Linda watched the well-rounded muscular body plunge into the surf. She admired Lola, whose marvellous body dripped with foam and cool sea. The woman came back to the water's edge and Linda saw how little she was covered by the scanty bikini. She appeared as a goddess coming from the sea with her long hair dripping and her svelte body outlined against the horizon. Oh, how she loved those buttocks, round and harmonious.

Instinctively Linda took Lola's hand.

"Let's take a dip together," Lola proposed.

Lola looked at her with the same fire that she had in the bedroom. A bizarre laughter crept over her lips and resounded in her superb chest as she brushed her long hair aside.

"You're still a virgin, isn't that so?" She didn't give Linda a chance to respond, but with one scoop of her hand she sprinkled the youngster with salt spray.

Linda was bewildered by the audacious question and she turned away to get a breath of air as another blast of sea water got her on the face and neck.

Finally she plunged in and the two swam together for a few yards. They gurgled and plopped around like two playful dolphins. They tickled each other and laughed and shouted like two happy children.

Lola had a powerful crawl stroke and she practically swam circles around little Linda. It was quite natural for Lola to be a good swimmer, Linda thought, for hadn't she the privilege of living by the sea eight months of the year? Linda showed her sportive best, and managed to do fairly well alongside the husky tanned siren.

They swam softly and evenly for about fifteen minutes. Lola noticed that Linda was tiring and she headed for shore. They reached another small inlet bordered by shrubs and deep-green pines. Lola waded ashore.

Linda staggered after her, completely out of breath, puffing happily.

"Say, you swim quickly."

"Not so badly." Lola responded modestly stretching her body from side to side to attain some warmth from the slightly cool air. The sun peeked out from a white passing cloud and appeared in the azure blue.

"How about some sun for awhile?"

Linda was already face down in the warm white sand. She watched her companion take off her bikini, shedding the two brief strips to reveal a torso completely browned with health-giving colour.

For a while, the adolescent couldn't take her eyes off the dark tanned nipples that extended at the end of Lola's ample breasts. Once her eyes did leave that fine proportion of bodily splendour, they roamed down to the triangle of hair that covered Lola's lower pelvis. It was light-brown and frizzled due to the sharp rays of the sun.

The tuft of hair gave her a marvellous animal quality. It demonstrated her vigour. Yes, the superb nest was her animal fur and it dripped with the last drops of the sea that melted on her warm, delicious torso.

The two women remained in the sun quietly. Not a word was spoken and they listened to the lapping sound of the surf.

Linda lay on her belly scanning the marvels of sun-worshipping Lola, who was stretched on her back in all her nude glory.

The young girl was surprised to see her own hand, as though guided by an unknown sorcerer, rubbing leisurely up against Lola's thigh.

Linda held her breath, but Lola didn't move. She wasn't sure if she was suffering from sunstroke or a rash impulse, but her hand kept moving along the thigh until it reached the borderline of Lola's pubic hair. She felt as though a wonderful current were passing through her fingers into the very veins of her body.

Boldly, Linda moved in on her friend who received her in her arms with a wide sensual smile. Suddenly the two women were startled by some voices coming from the brush.

Linda sprung to her feet, her face red with shame. Had someone seen them together? She was still inhibited by her bourgeois education. Lola merely looked around tranquilly while seated on her fabulous rear and two elbows.

"That's probably Robert and Alice. They really are like two overheated dogs the way they go at it." She seemed to visualize the young couple as an engaging smile formed around her mouth. "What are they doing back there?" Linda suspected what they may be doing, but she wanted to hear it from Lola's own lips.

"But, my dear, it's quite simple. Robert is just fornicating with our adorable maid. I must say that for a boy of his age he isn't lacking in certain qualities. As for that matter, Alice isn't either."

She giggled and smiled as she listened to the muffled voices with their effortless moans from behind the foliage.

Linda was dumbstruck and she couldn't find the courage to return to the outstretched position she had taken on the warm, form-fitting sand. Lola jerked her head up at once and concluded:

"Come along, we'll surprise them. The naughty children. For shame." She sprung to her legs with a teasing expression on her face.

She took Linda by the hand and practically dragged her by force to the wooded area. Linda followed like someone in a lethargic state, who vaguely has the sensation that something strange is going to happen.

At the brink of the pines, Lola pointed to a spot that was encircled by brush. She put her finger to her lips to signify that she wished the utmost silence. They both tip-toed forward cautiously, moving in on their objective.

All at once Lola threw herself to the ground as though she were performing a military manoeuvre. Linda imitated her, even though she was startled and rather fed up with the total aurora of secrecy.

Then through a clump of thinned-out bushes, she managed

to see Robert and a winsome young girl in an odd position for two youngsters such as they. Lola was right. They were behaving in a most obscene fashion. Robert was straddling the girl as though she were a dog or something. Linda was surprised to see her on all fours. Robert was merciless in his push-pull, cork-snapping movements. The young maid emitted several cries. It was difficult for Linda to distinguish whether those cries were of pain or of pleasure.

Linda was transfixed to the spot. She was positively excited by these new erotic scenes. She said to herself that they were devastating, to say the least. With her right hand she brushed some drool away from her lips. Lola noticed her gesture and almost began to laugh.

"But he's putting it..." Lola covered her mouth to keep her voice under control.

"No, my pet. He isn't buggering her, as your boyfriends in London probably use the term, he's making love to her roman fashion. Of course, you don't know what that is?"

Lola gingerly stripped Linda of her bikini. Linda was perplexed. It was impossible for her to cry out for fear of disturbing the others. Oh, what a ridiculous situation she was in. But the adept hands of the undulating Lola brought about a new perspective to her limited horizons. When Linda turned to reproach her friend, she remarked that Lola's eyes were almost blood-shot. It had come about all of sudden as though she were stricken by some unknown condition – or passion.

Her hand went straight to Linda's pussy and the tips of her long supple fingers worked miracles in that lubricious region. Soon she had Linda panting and straining to keep from being found out by Robert and Alice. But anyway, they were humming their own tune, and it is a hundred to one that they would have heard.

Linda let herself be masturbated while looking onto the magnificent show in front of her. Good naturedly she thought of Lola. Poor Lola was being left out. So Linda, thoughtful and courteous, placed her trembling hand down on the curly blossom that thinned out at her companion's belly. The two women began to masturbate each other slowly, while watching a pair of minors screw with the rhythm of perfect professionals.

It wasn't long before Linda felt a wave of pleasure descend upon her. She sensed a multitude of warm prickly thrills invade her wet sex, which was carefully being explored by the diligent Lola.

She started to groan, but held back as best she could. Her teeth were sealed together. *Do unto others as you would have them do unto you.* The proverb took life and Linda gently fingered her impetuous companion.

Lola's thighs were divine. They were the thighs of a woman who was voluptuous and mighty. Linda did not feel disgusted by the act, which surprised her no end. Abstractly, if she had thought it over when alone, she would have berated herself a thousand times for being so low and uncouth, but this very real performance delighted her. She clutched at the thighs.

Lola licked the adolescent's belly all over, and then her big mouth hovered in the region of the breasts. The lips nipped at the left teat and then opened wide and engulfed the defenceless breast.

The husky woman sucked on one nipple and fingered the other. Then she switched over, and this excited Linda to the point where she thought, she thought... well she didn't think, she just drifted into a vague emulsion of sensations. She could not say where she was or why, or what she was doing. The young girl's eyes rolled in her head like two agates would in a pin-ball machine.

Her teats were being licked, sucked and massaged frenetically, while on the other side of the bush Robert and his little waif ignored the nearby presence of the passionate intruders.

The two teenagers were well on their way to reaching a paroxysm stemming from their rife and energetic gestures. They were coupled together like two little puppies who have just learned to screw and are highly delighted with their find.

To and fro they rocked, and Alice got wetter and wetter, and Robert, the active one, got hotter and bigger. It was just a matter of seconds now. Then the cataclysm erupted. Robert felt the veins in his stiff cock shake with panic. His loins swelled and the head of his penis dribbled its first throbs of white liquid. Alice felt heat in the region of her vagina. A heat that stirred a melting pot of wild sensations. She was building up to the explosion.

Robert inundated her pussy with spunk, and the soaking hole pressed back and forth, clenching and throbbing like an underground earthquake. Curly-headed Alice flopped to the ground, her head crashing in the sand under the weight of the fatigued lad. A thin thread of saliva poured from her mouth and trickled down her chin.

Linda puffed and gritted her teeth and let out an *ohhhhh... ahhhhh...* that would have been heard by the others if they had not been so tired and *ohhing* and *ahhing* themselves in the last throes of orgasm. A viscous fluid flowed from Linda's hot, wet pussy. It trickled down her thigh unerringly to the sand, which thirstily absorbed the juice of her first real sexual climax.

Lola, the silent one, had come twice. Elegant, discreet and seeking pleasure at every turn, she held her joy for herself. Perhaps she even longed for a third orgasm as her head buried itself between Linda's thighs. A tongue snaked out and lapped up the delicious nectar of the young girl, who was barely recovering her wits.

Linda watched Robert and Alice through her dream-weary eyes.

"Oh, Robert, my lovely boy." Alice's voice was shaky and she had difficulty getting her wind back.

And the little maid wasn't even looking at her handsome knight with his pink cock growing soft. He was flat on his back exhausted, and she was lying face down. But this awkward position didn't prevent her from toying with his limp dick.

"Now, what's the matter? Haven't you had enough? I'm going in the water."

"Oh, you're awful," Alice chided. "When you've had it and no longer want it, everyone else has to cede to his highness. It isn't fair."

"But that's not true, my little sweet. You can always get it *somewhere* in our household. Isn't there Lola or uncle to do you justice?" He struggled to a sitting position.

Linda turned toward Lola and her face showed a questioning perplexity. Lola simply smiled and stroked her hair.

"Your uncle? Why, I had him on top of me all night..." sighed Alice.

"And you didn't like it?" asked Robert.

"I'm not talking about that. But I prefer you, and I know whom you prefer. It's Lola. Just because she is more experienced and knows too much for her own good... And now your cousin Linda has arrived. You'll probably be after her, won't you?"

Linda listened attentively. She fidgeted behind the leafy

plants, earnestly waiting for Robert's answer.

"Who, Linda? Come to think of it, I'd like to get to her before my uncle does. It would be funny, that." He laughed aloud. "Just think, and she's a virgin too."

"She's not bad," admitted Alice.

"Very nicely built, to tell the truth." Robert contemplated his future victim. That is, he saw her in his mind's eye and hadn't the slightest idea that she was hearing every word, flat on her belly a few yards away.

Linda turned red. Only she could know how to take his remarks. Was it a pleasant compliment, or did she feel annoyed? Time was to judge – and witness an impending scene.

Lola and Linda snuck away as silently as they had arrived. Both were feeling the wear and tear of their little peek-a-boo session. Yet neither regretted it, by the happy smile that flushed on their faces.

♦

An hour later in her room, Linda began to think. She sat on the edge of her bed and nibbled her nails.

Lola knocked on the door and informed Linda that lunch was not a very common thing at the villa. When one got hungry, he or she might take the lunch where ever he or she desired. She told Linda that uncle Arthur usually ate lunch in the library, where he worked on his latest novel until midnight.

"Arthur is a real recluse. He hates to see people during the day," Lola confided to Linda. "He takes a morning swim very early and then he closes himself off from the rest of the world in his sanctuary. If he wants something," she added with a bewitching smile, "he just rings. I'll bring you your lunch right here in your room, if you wish?"

Linda nodded that it would be very kind of her to take such pains. Lola assured her that it would make her happy to be of service to such a pretty newcomer to the 'establishment'. She was out of the room in a jiffy.

The adolescent, once more alone, tried to gather the remnants of her thoughts regarding the near hallucinatory events of that morning.

What troubled her the most was what Robert had said, about seeing who would get her first, he or his uncle. He was perhaps only kidding...

Linda hadn't seen her uncle yet, but Lola told her he kept to himself during the daytime. She was sure her uncle, who hadn't seen her for years, would cut a more interesting figure than that whelping conceited pup, Robert. But then again, uncle Arthur had Lola. At least that's what Alice said... And yet Lola apparently didn't care about these strange, amorous deviations.

Linda was lost, utterly lost in her thoughts, which seemed to get more entangled as she strained her pretty head when somebody knocked on the door.

"Come in," she said cheerily, thinking it would be Lola. The young girl wore only a pyjama top and had nothing to fear since the intimate barriers with Lola had been broken down.

The door opened – and Robert entered. Linda jumped off her bed and instinctively grabbed her pyjama top and clutched it to her chest and stomach to conceal her semi-nudity.

"Well here you are miss... cold cuts, salad, fruit, milk, bread and butter and banana cream pie. Doesn't that look good?"

"I thought Lola was going to bring me my lunch."

"Oh, I'm sorry. Lola is busy for the moment. Uncle Arthur wanted to see her. I thought, well, maybe we could lunch together. That way, we could get to know each other better."

Linda was suspicious of her cousin. Something ironic and suggestive sparkled in his young face.

"You mean we should eat here?" Linda questioned Robert.

"Why not?" Robert affirmed the decision by shutting the door behind him.

He put the tray on the floor and sat besides Linda. The young girl didn't move. She now knew too well what might follow. No, dear sweet cousin Robert didn't come up to just have lunch with her! She had no time to really reflect if the idea pleased her or not. She was quivering with emotion and that was the one thing she was aware of, just that and no more.

"You know it's a shame that we haven't gotten together before. Our family is really just about as scattered as leaves in the wind." Robert was trying to make conversation. Even with his cynical attitude and his budding knowledge of certain amorous pursuits, precociously developed, Robert obviously had little imagination when it came to seducing a girl. He was too classic in his approach. This is what Linda felt as she waited for the attack.

She was amused in a way. An idea flashed through her head. There was no sense in sitting there numb and blustered by this whole nonsense. She might as well play a part and really have fun. After all, she knew what the score was. She got up from the bed and paraded toward the window. Her pyjama top just barely covered her dainty buttocks. Linda made sure that she wiggled her hips provocatively.

"Sometimes it isn't wise to meet so early. Young people are rarely interesting," Linda teased as she pulled the curtain to one side.

"You mean you prefer older men. Well, it's my opinion..."
She didn't give him a chance to finish.

"I only mean what I said," Linda retorted haughtily as she leaned her head close to the window pane, as though interested in something not too far away. "What do you say we have some lunch. I'm starved."

"Starved for what?" Robert said sardonically.

Linda turned around and was startled to see Robert lounging on her bed. The horrid fellow had taken off his bathing trunks and his cock was protruding in the air. His eyes never left the lower part of Linda's fine torso.

"I couldn't help it. It's your rear that did it, honestly," The boy confessed.

"Well you've got a nerve." She looked at him, half-angrily and half-amusedly. Linda noticed the size of the penis that stuck rigidly up between his legs.

"You're not going to tell me that this is the first time you've ever seen a man nude?" He was cocky, and extremely sure of himself. "Come here and have a closer look. No-one is going to bite you."

She didn't feel like being intimidated by a mere boy who was two years younger than she. She strode over to the bed, trying to lend grown-up poise to her young age.

Robert grabbed her by the hand and drew her to the bed. "Take a good look at it. Not bad. Don't you like it?"

She did, but she wasn't going to say so. The whole

procedure was wicked and entirely out of order.

"You think you're smart, don't you? Well, you're not a man even if you think you are. And with that thing, that small pencil you're so proud of..."

Suddenly he gripped her by the waist and she found her head two inches away from his glaring glans.

"That's the way I like to see you. Fresh and cocky like me. I can't take little girls that cry and give in."

She began to kick and fuss. She tried to struggle loose, but the boy held a firm grip. Robert was strong for his age. He lifted weights and swam all summer, thus his strength was much greater than hers.

"You are a real brat." She pounded on his chest and scratched his thighs. They wrestled on the bed like two young kittens. Linda had no idea that her pyjama top had fallen open and her body was exposed to her youthful assailant.

He exhausted her to the point where she was feeling the struggle dissipate in her limbs. A new sensation crept through her. A new, sensual feeling took possession of the young girl and slowly she submitted to the know-how and ardent desire of the youth.

There was no use shaming. She let herself go and abandoned herself to the zealous young Robert.

He hastened to put his lips to her multiple splendours. He kissed her pussy, her musky armpits, and her pert breasts. Suddenly she threw her arms around her cousin, half in submission and half in desire. She looked at him curiously as his mouth moved toward hers.

"Oh, Robert. What am I supposed to do?"

"Don't be a shrew. Kiss me, first of all."

They arched over the bed quilt in a long embrace. Their tongues entwined like two seething serpents while four hands moved quickly, impetuously, over their locked bodies.

Linda felt her cousin's hardened cock and a burst of feverish enthusiasm went to her head. Robert moved away from her, and for a moment she thought perhaps she had insulted him somehow in her ecstatic state of mind and body.

"And now, you're going to kiss it. Aren't you?" He wasn't asking. He was commanding.

"Yes. I want to kiss it. And I want to have it in my mouth,

it's so handsome..." The young girl lowered her head toward the object of her admiration, taking the member between her lips. She sipped on the head of Robert's rampant penis. An unescapable odour went to her head and she was drunk with delight for many minutes after.

"With your tongue." Robert breathed heavily; Linda began to lick his cock gently up and down the shaft. *It tastes like salt,* she thought, and then she placed a good part of its length it in her mouth. Robert moaned and put his hands on her head. Linda was sucking him steadily and her tongue was active, heightening his pleasure.

Instinctively Linda pivoted so her thighs were near her cousin's head. She awaited Robert's initiative. It wasn't long before the panting lad had plunged his tongue into Linda's quivering cunt. His tonguing was more diverse and stronger than Linda's. The combination of his sexual response and her growing appetite worked wonders, and the two writhed with violent caresses.

Linda thought she was going to go mad with excitement. She nibbled at Robert's testicles, which hung down like two ripe fruit. She felt a certain charge shoot through the boy's body. He jumped violently and stiffened a bit.

"STOP, stop, or I'll come!" he cried.

Linda was disconcerted, with her mouth opened, not daring to recommence her voluptuous act. She was embarrassed and annoyed by this brusque interruption. But already Robert was leaning down and caressing her hair.

"I want this to be on you. Or more precisely inside you. Now we're going to make love together. Haven't you ever done it before?"

"N... N... No, never," stammered Linda.

But Robert wasn't listening. With one hand he spread her legs apart and slipped his cock inside her wet crack. He hadn't gone far when Linda's eyes bulged widely. But Robert pressed forward brutally. He had every intention of ripping home.

The young girl cried shrilly. She felt as though she were being knifed in two. A tear rolled down her cheek.

"Don't cry," murmured Robert... "Now you're no longer a virgin. Look, see. You're a grown-up now."

Linda felt a trickle run down her thighs. She feebly looked

down at her shapely leg and saw a streak of blood flow irregularly along her soft skin.

"It hurts. Oh, what pain I feel." She was in tears out of suffering, out of shame and out of the sight of blood.

The boy withdrew his penis almost completely.

But it was only to dig it in farther. Linda let out a suffocating cry, but strangely enough the pain had dissolved and a sudden pleasure was enthralling her very being. A soft wave of sweet delight spread through her belly and fired her vulva. Robert meanwhile moved like a piston, well greased by the mixture of liquids that were pouring out of the depucelated virgin.

With each movement, Linda sighed her acquiesence to the handsome Robert. Welcoming every stroke, she felt her pleasure augmenting and she gripped Robert with all her strength as if she were afraid that the mounting joy would cease.

"Faster, faster Robert." She begged him to pulverize her bruised pussy. Then stars burst in front of her wobbly, dizzy head. A nebula of a thousand flames ignited, and she was at that glorious climax where the body plunges into a boiling pool of endless delights. Her movements now were quick and frantic, as though she were trying to prolong her ecstasy forever. Her lover dug into her to the root and ejaculated his hot sperm in a thick column. Linda felt the influx of the liquid and she contracted her muscles in order to milk dry his spasming cock.

They had matched one orgasm against the other. They had come together, as though they had been doing this sort of thing for years.

Linda let her legs fall apart, and she was totally free from shame. Later on, this attitude so deliberate in its manifestation surprised her and yet gave her a peculiar and new sense of pride.

Robert lay on top of her, quite fatigued. He had emptied himself like a trouper and he sprawled disjointedly over the limp form of his naked cousin.

A few minutes passed by, long and slumbersome. Linda slowly returned to reality as she disengaged herself from post-orgasmic torpor. She opened her eyes and the first thing she saw was Robert's lips crawling toward her cheek.

"How was it?" He smiled and wriggled into a better position with his head on her shoulder. "The act of love isn't too bad, is it?"

"It's marvellous," replied Linda, who had tasted its pangs and happiness for the first time. "I never thought it could be like this. It is so sweet and sensual."

She stretched like a young kitten and her arms locked at the elbows. Her hands joined at the back of Robert's neck where her fingers spread through his curly hair.

"You know it's funny," Robert grinned and pecked her on the forehead... "It's the first time you've made love, and it's the first time that I've ever made love... with a virgin. That's funny isn't it?"

Linda wanted to know what it was like. Perhaps he wasn't satisfied. She had not really thought of what it was like for him; she had just experienced a thrilling ordeal, topped with the cream of pleasure.

"Was it any different?" She tried to catch his eyes.

"I'm not complaining. But listen, my dear cousin, you'll have to watch yourself here, and be cautious." Robert looked seriously at her.

She put her hand down toward her pussy and tried to keep the thick mixture of blood and sperm from staining the bedspread.

"Be cautious? Of what?" She seemed puzzled and really wanted to know what on earth he meant by all this.

"Come closer and I'll explain..."

At that precise moment the door opened and the two moved apart as Lola tip-toed into the room. The dark-skinned woman looked half-amused and half-serious. Linda didn't know how to take her, let alone how to act or find words to mutter.

She had forgotten that Lola would come back and she was taken aback by the unwanted apparition. She tried to crawl into bed as though she were trying to hide some evidence. Of course, it was of no avail, for the evidence was undisputedly in front of Lola. Robert didn't budge and Linda was astonished to see how casually he treated the whole affair.

He simply turned his head nonchalantly and said to the mistress (for Linda imagined her to be one):

"You're right in time to accompany her to the bathroom. That's a woman's duty, you know?"

Lola helped Linda out of bed as though she were ready to spank a naughty child. As Linda scrambled to her feet, Lola teased her ironically.

"Come along. We have to clean up. Now, aren't you a bad girl, so terribly pressed for it... Tsk, tsk, tsk... Ah, what a family." They reached the bathroom and Linda was suddenly downcast and felt certain recriminations. Lola was less talkative and scolding, but managed to add a few words.

"We'll have to hurry. After I soak you, you'll have to get dressed quickly. Your uncle wants to see you and say... *hello*."

chapter two

A half an hour later Linda was seated in the salon waiting for her uncle. Lola had left her there, for she was busy in the kitchen preparing the night's dinner. Robert seemed to have disappeared all of a sudden. And as for all that, Alice, the maid, was no where to be seen.

The young girl felt tired, her head swimming in the clouds. She didn't realize it but she was suffering from the fatigue of love. However, a smile mounted to her lips while thinking of what she had just accomplished with Robert. Oh well, her virginity was something in the past. She wouldn't be able to use *that* as a defense for many valuable reasons. But Linda truly didn't have any regrets, since she had made a discovery that was altogether agreeable.

She was a woman now – well almost. It would be better to say that she was on the road to becoming one. Her imagination got the better of her. She wondered when her cousin would make love to her again. Maybe he would come into her room that night? In that case, she would remember not to lock the door. *Perhaps it will be Lola who will start up again?* Oh well, she would just have to wait and see what would happen... Her reverie was interrupted by footsteps coming from the library. The door opened and a man entered the salon. He approached with a smiling, delightful air.

"Ah, Linda. How good it is to see you. How are you? I'm glad to see you among us."

It was uncle Arthur alright. Linda noticed quickly, as he strutted across the room, his elegant walk and perfect masculine bearing. He was tall, sun-tanned, athletic with steel-grey eyes and greying temples. Uncle Arthur was exactly the type of man Linda thought of as being the perfect seducer. She even remembered him from her younger days. This splendid hunk of manhood had not changed. And maybe he had even improved. She found him very attractive. She greeted him with a timid strained voice as she put out her hand to be grasped warmly by the distinguished Arthur.

But Arthur paid no attention to the outstretched hand and he took the girl by her shoulders and kissed her lightly on the corner of the mouth. Linda turned beet-red as she inhaled the lavender perfume emanating from the tall man, who despite her blushing, was only her uncle.

Arthur looked her over, his hands never leaving her shoulders. He smiled.

"Well then. It is really wonderful to see you. You've gotten quite attractive, you know? Well, well, well... How do you like our house?"

"Oh, it's fine," Linda exclaimed. "I met Lola and Robert and we... and we..." She didn't know how to end her sentence. Was it possible that uncle Arthur knew how they had spent the morning and early afternoon?

"Let's just say that you got along fine together." Arthur helped her disentangle the sentence and straighten her thoughts out. Little did he know she was thinking quite well. It was only manipulating in a proper manner that concerned her.

"Tell me Linda? I know this is unusual to ask, especially the day of your arrival, but could you help me out? Lola is busy and Robert, well that rascal can never he found when someone wants him. You won't mind will you?" He smiled graciously.

"Not at all. But I don't know whether I shall be capable of doing what you wish. What is it, may I ask?"

"Oh, there's no mystery to it. I'll explain. Just follow me into the library."

Uncle Arthur led the way into the library taking long sure strides. Linda followed obediently. The library was paneled by dark mahogany. There were many books in the bookcases which ran across the room. She knew Arthur was highly literate and intellectual and she felt that she should watch every word. The windows were large and bordered by red-velvet curtains with a strip of white mousseline running down the edges.

The curtains filtered the bright sun and the room bathed its few pieces of furniture, a great table covered with papers, a large ample armchair, a divan in a melody of soft brooding colours.

Linda noticed a ladder which led to the stacks of books on

the upper shelves.

"We'll here it is. My hide-away where I work. All you will have to do is bring the books I name so that I shall be able to take notes. That's easy enough isn't?"

"I think I'll be able to manage that alright." Linda laughed, apparently at ease for the first time. She was beginning to find her uncle warm and pleasing.

"How will I go about finding the book you want?" she asked, glancing at the many many shelves of literature.

"I have a method so don't worry about it. All the cases are marked alphabetically."

They began to work and Linda found that the job was easy and not bone-breaking at all. The only thing that presented a problem was climbing up and down the ladder. She wished that she had worn some slacks. It was embarrassing for her to climb that ladder with her legs pinched together.

"I can't find it," she declared, leaning far to the right and then to the left.

"Wait I'll help you," Arthur said courteously, rising from his armchair and moving to where she was.

Linda continued to look for the misplaced book, while below, her uncle gazed up her skirt, which was large enough to give the spectator a languorous view. The girl turned around and pretended to still be searching for the book, but she felt the penetrating glance of uncle Arthur and this unsettled her nerves. She was forced to keep her legs slightly apart to keep from losing her balance.

"You're right. I think I left that book in my apartment in the city. You can come down now." Arthur helped her to the ground as his strong fingers gripped her waist. She felt a chill run up her spine as his hands slid up to her bosom. When she turned around, she felt guilty for having such a horrid imagination.

Uncle Arthur thumbed his chin and murmured a few words.

"You are very pretty, my lovely niece, and you were particularly attractive on that ladder. I must admit that you have splendid legs. It makes me realize that you have really grown up. It's silly of me not to have thought of it before."

She was flattered, turned red and spun in a half-turn. Linda knew these gestures were unbecoming of a 'grown-up'. Yet the presence of her uncle so close and his constant attention instilled a new sensation far different from the one she felt with Robert.

Uncle Arthur moved toward his desk. With his right hand outstretched he indicated a chair.

"Sit down Linda."

He scratched his head and it was evident that another idea was brewing in his intellectual mind.

"Better yet. Come and sit on the arm of my chair."

Linda's head bobbed up at this strange request. She flushed crimson with timidity.

"Come along and be friendly."

"Do you want me so close?"

"Of course." Arthur's smile had won her over. She had no choice but to have confidence in this handsome man who was, after all, her uncle.

Once seated, Arthur put his arm around her waist. And before she had a chance to jerk away, he had another hand half up her skirt where he was patting her thighs. Linda was troubled and she stiffened partly out of surprise and partly out of fright.

"I think it would be better if I left now," she murmured entirely without conviction. The poor youngster didn't want to disobey and yet...

As though he had not heard her remark, her uncle exclaimed in a vigorous tone: "You're not comfortable kicking around like that."

He was peculiar. Linda noticed it for the first time. His lips screwed up and his eyes grew feverish and even to a young girl as youthful as Linda, she knew it was the outward signs of lust. He became eager and restless and his tongue rolled over the corner of his mouth.

She had found that he had greatly changed in the span of just a few minutes. He was a veritable Jekyll and Hyde case, but there was something amazingly attractive about him. His golden tan flushed and gave him added colour. His grey temples marked him as very masculine and resolved. Arthur's sinuous and strong arms were commanding and sure, despite their unleashed nervous energy, in grasping and capturing the delicious morsel who had come to live in his house.

Linda felt his warm breath behind her neck, between her

hair and running lightly down her back. His hand roamed under her slip and toyfully tickled her pubic hair. Linda sensed a great probing thing throbbing near her asshole. He seemed to be juggling her on his lap as though he wanted to rip through her clothes. His member was violently searching, and for some reason she pictured a madman with a hammer.

Uncle Arthur almost wrenched the breath out her with his forceful grasp. When she turned to express her disapproval, she met a pair of eyes that glittered with fierce heat. She was spellbound and strangely enough attracted by this new face she saw. Her uncle almost foamed at the mouth as his right hand busied itself with the task of unbuttoning his trousers.

Linda almost leapt up but she was held fast. When she looked down at his lap a huge penis, rigidly erect, poked in the air. She had never seen anything like it. It was twice as big as Robert's both in length and diameter. She watched the purple head of this proud cock, with its slight opening. It pushed itself towards her face as though it were a canon ready to fire. Of course, she instinctively moved backward, but her uncle held her prisoner in his armchair. A lustful smile, triumphal and wicked, crinkled his face.

"Well, what do you have to say now, my little one? It's big and handsome. Isn't it nicer than the one that you put between your legs a little while ago with that untamed rascal Robert? But, by heck, I think your afraid. Why? It isn't going to hurt you, little dear. You'll have it anyway, and you'll be so happy about it when we're finished that I even think you'll ask for more of it. What do you think of that?"

While he was speaking, he was already caressing the open mouth of the young girl. It appeared as though she had already abandoned any idea of resisting she might have had. Linda leaned forward and gently nibbled on the head of Arthur's penis, which had a strong odour that excited her. Her teeth inspired her uncle to grow even harder.

She had *some* experience... just that bit from the morning. And Linda planned on using it all. She remembered that Robert told her to use her tongue first of all, which she did, spiralling around the massive prick in barber-pole fashion. Her uncle plunged his weapon in her mouth as though it were made of rubber. Poor Linda almost suffocated.

"You like it, don't you?" he asked, a rhetorical question. His mood and excitement were so great that his powerful thrusts had Linda's face all red and her eyes closed to keep tears from flowing. Never had she endured such a ruthless attack.

"Suck well, my girl. Go on, do it well."

Defenceless Linda could hardly breathe, let alone answer back to the rampaging adult who, horror of horrors, was her uncle. Try as she would she could not get all of that phallus in her mouth, but she found energy enough to take as much in as she could and licked it clean with her flickering tongue. With a tremendous effort she was able to stretch her lips about half-way down the thick shaft. One of her hands was then guided to the spot where bristling pubic hairs, black as night, hid a pair of balls as large as lemons. Her hand cupped the heavy testicles and her trembling fingers began to stroke and massage them.

With various movements of her head, up and down and from side to side, she began to masturbate her uncle with mouth and tongue. Linda felt the veins in his cock throb and expand. The sudden expansion excited the girl and she became more and more audacious. Her hand grasped Arthur's penis as though she had been acquainted with it for a long time, and her tongue darted around the purple glans, which was oozing a thick white liquid ever so slowly. Linda began to bite on it as though it were good enough to eat.

Then his cock began to pulsate with a sudden spasm, and before Linda could think of what she might do under such circumstances, her mouth was full of salty, burning fluid which drooled from her bottom lip. She looked up bewildered and flushed. Uncle Arthur placed his hand over her mouth, preventing her from spitting it out. So it went down swallowed, mouthful after mouthful. It was strange to see the girl brimming over with his hot jism – there must have been a pint of it, or so it seemed.

Linda did not seem unpleased with the taste of Arthur's come. She even went back to suckling the phallus greedily, trying to get the last white drops out of it. It was though she were a baby calf trying to get at the dripping remainders of mother's milk.

When her feast finally came to a halt, she drew back and took a good look at the man, who was dropping in his armchair with limbs akimbo and his eyes half-closed in delirium.

"Little wench. You had me in the stars for awhile. I had no idea you were so handy with that lovely mouth of yours. And did you enjoy it?"

What could she say? She blushed, her eyes could not meet his inflamed eyes and so they remained downcast. The act had been accomplished and words, she thought, were useless. However, she managed to utter a few wise ones.

"If it pleased you uncle, it had the same effect on me."

They sat quietly for a few minutes and then Arthur's hand began to wander up Linda's thighs in the same direction. This time he pinched at her bottom and his finger came to rest on the pink rim of her asshole.

"No, don't touch *tonton!*" She jumped up and ran to the window. "Please don't touch it."

Arthur wondered about his niece. What was this 'tonton' business? Did she have an anal complex? He planned on finding out. He strode over to the door and locked it. When he came back to the centre of the room, Linda was sitting on the table, her bare legs offering an attractive sight.

"And now my darling, you're going to see something that will perhaps shock you and rob you of that snippy and carefree attitude you have." His voice grew hard and his lips turned cruel with a mocking air.

When Linda saw him close the door and lock it, she had already suspected that something unpleasant was in store for her. She thought of screaming out, but there was no one who would come to her rescue. But on second thought, what more could he do to her? She was too nervous to appreciate the situation for what it was worth.

Her uncle did not even take the trouble of placing his drooping cock back in his trousers. He walked to the window and closed the curtains and then came back to her.

"I was told that you were 'devirginized' this morning. It was just what I wanted to do myself. I was counting on it – but one can't have everything. In any case, there are parts of you that are still intact, and healthy, and virgin. Robert wouldn't have operated in two directions. There is a limit to the young lad's experience."

He noticed that Linda didn't catch on to what he was saying. He quickly put his hands on her legs and pulled aside her skirt. Uncle Arthur was in complete control of himself this time.

"I am speaking, my dear cousin, in terms that you will understand better... I am speaking of your 'virginal anus'."

Linda put her hand over her mouth in an effort to hold back a stifling cry.

"My what?"

"Yes, exactly, my dear. And I promise you that you will not get out of this room before you have given me your little flower of a hot pink asshole. I want *some* sort of pleasure today. Quick, get undressed."

Arthur had already unbuttoned his shirt. He rapidly peeled off his pants and shorts, preparing for what was almost a daily practice with him in his adult life.

Her uncle revealed two strong legs and a muscular torso. His chest was covered with dark crinkly hair the same colour as that outlined his huge sex organs. As he eyed Linda, who was undressing slowly with a contorted expression on her face, his cock bolted up like a flag-pole. In a few seconds his prick had once more taken on the respectable proportions of the last half-hour.

Linda seemed drained of all thoughts, and had no pluck to fight back with. She was incapable of making a gesture. Arthur's fierce eyes burnt right through her while the same cruel mouth twisted in delight and terrible passion.

"Ah, you don't want to behave, is that it? Well, we shall see about that. I'll have you just the same!"

She had not as yet taken off her blouse and Arthur, with one fell swoop of his large hand, ripped it from her body. Her eyes almost popped out of their sockets when he then did the same with her bra. Linda's pert breasts quivered in the air. Wild and hungry, uncle Arthur pounced on her and mercilessly bit into those two ripe fruits.

Linda felt the teeth marks and she cried out in pain. The sudden burst brought him back to his senses and he let up for an instant, looking strangely at the girl who dared to defy him.

With a thrust of his hand he ripped off her skirt, then put his fingers around the elastic waistband of her panties and snapped the cord, ripping flimsy material.

Linda was now completely nude. Her uncle leaned heavily on her, forcing her to arch over the table.

His weight and extreme passion crushed her and she felt the jabs of the many items that were scattered on the table. Bites and kisses were bestowed upon her mouth, neck, and breasts. Then uncle Arthur backed off for awhile and contemplated his victim.

"She's well-made, my little niece!" He laughed, speaking to himself. "Is she really a woman now? Do you know what one does to delicious little girls like you?"

With one hand he pushed her legs apart, and stabbed a finger brutally in her anus. Linda squealed, but her uncle pushed harder with his finger, pushing into her.

"Now, don't scream." He rubbed his cock against her belly. It was as hard as a policeman's baton. "What are you going to do when you have *this* up there?" He emphasised his words by applying pressure with his buried finger.

Linda screeched an 'ouch'. She was horrified by the thought that his big instrument would pulverize her tender rose-bud. Even a finger hurt as it went back and forth. What would an enormous piston like his do to her? The idea made her faint. She spread her legs wider apart to relieve the pressure of the thick finger. Pleasure mixed with pain ebbed in the cells of her lower body. The tickling sensation close to her vulva was undeniable, agreeable in some ways though it plugged up her very tiny aperture. "You're beginning to like it, aren't you? Very well."

He withdrew his finger and inhaled with satisfaction.

"Come here. We're going to do it on the divan." He led her by her rump, which she found embarrassing to say the least.

He lay her on the soft divan. Linda felt the rigid cock against her body and awaited the tormenting moment, the moment when he would penetrate. She was sure he would be brutal about it, and it would all come about when she was least prepared for it. He was jealous of what Robert had accomplished with her and he wanted to be one up on his loathsome nephew.

She sensed his preparation, his heat and his terrifying, throbbing member. Then he leaned over his niece and urged her to open her thighs. She obeyed and watched his face sink like the sun as it buried itself in her pussy. His hot tongue soothed her cunt lips, which had been bruised by the assaults of cousin Robert. It was the first time she realized that this area still hurt.

Then he put his mouth at her anus, and penetrated with the

tip of his tongue. Uncle Arthur was full of improvisations. She hoped that he meant his tongue and not his thing. Linda prayed that he would reconsider his terrible plan.

What he was doing to her now proved to be entirely to her liking. He licked around the rim and then tongued slightly in the hole like a timid bee. It sent chills of warm delight up and down her spine. She even enjoyed the chiding bites on her rump that caused her to squirm. Linda wiggled her buttocks, spreading wider in order to please her uncle, whom she hoped would spare her.

Arthur was drunk with the intoxication of love. He began to lick her furiously. Both the vagina and anus were neatly combed by his unfailing tongue, but the anus was particularly favoured.

Linda started to moan with pleasure. It felt good, but really good. Squeals of animal delight issued from her wet lips.

"Do you like that?" cried Arthur, with his face buried between her musky buttocks.

"Oh, that's fine," murmured the ecstatic youngster. "It's delicious. I love it so much."

The uncle remained spellbound as though he were contemplating two gorgeous hunks of fruit. He squeezed the buttocks as though he wanted to rip them off.

"And now comes the fun. We are going to see whether you'll like what I am going to do."

Linda's mind reeled in a mad attempt to ward off what might be a true disaster. A sudden thought occurred to her. Perhaps he would be less brutal if she pretended that she wanted it as much as he. He might lose interest. It was worth taking the chance, for she had nothing more to lose.

"Do what you like... You can do whatever you choose, uncle dear." Somehow her voice sounded unassured and weak.

He waited for nothing more. He had the permission – and even if he hadn't it would have amounted to the same thing. Arthur turned her over on her belly, and her head was quickly buried in between her knees. Through her spread out legs she was able to see the enormous cock wend its way toward her rump. It rolled around as though it were getting its bearing and then it stiffened in aim and finality of purpose. At that moment Linda knew she was doomed. She closed her eyes and breathed heavily. Instinctively she recoiled and tried to dodge his thrust, but it was too late. He had already lodged the head of his cock in the tiny wet opening. A tear fell from the cheek of the unlucky adolescent. Arthur noticed the whimpering of his child-like niece, but it made no difference to his operations. He attacked for a second time, lubricating the anus with more saliva and an adept finger, easing it open. "You see, little doll, you'll never be a real woman until you're deflowered right here. It may just as well be me..."

And he proved what he meant. With one heave he burst through that tight band of flesh and into the entrails of his beloved niece. Linda let out a savage howl. She had never felt such a painful sensation before. It was a profound suffering that caught in her throat. A staff of masculine flesh had broken through her sphincter with all the animal force needed to rupture a tiny, undefended aperture.

Thoughts spun in her broken head. *That's not the way one makes love. He's trying to kill me.* Her body remained pinned to the divan, with her thighs spread wide apart and her face tormented and crushed on the pillow. Linda was in a stupor. The only reaction and return to life she could muster up was repulsion toward her uncle's biting embraces on the neck and his teeth marks against her mouth. He was horrid to her, she mused. Who could have such a wicked, monstrous uncle?

Uncle Arthur was only half inside the small opening. He still had his work cut out, so to speak, and he was never one who shirked a task, whether it was literature or love. For this man both of them intertwined, and drained his very senses.

He plunged once more, only more brutally, more indecently. Stretching her red, glistening ring to breaking-point, he managed to bury his prick to the hilt in the stricken girl, who seemed to bob and remain paralysed with her neck stretching taut and her eyelids tightly closed.

The grey-templed man accelerated his thrusts while he played with the wet-lipped cunt of his lovely niece. Linda was unaware, due to the violent pain, that she had two rectal orgasms. Only during the second one did the element of pleasure begin to enter into play. A strange smile crept over her like a light veil of soft silk.

Her uncle rolled on her like a rough sea captain, his pleasure as immense as the ocean and as joyous as a sky of deep azure.

"Tell me, Linda, does it still hurt? I think you are beginning to enjoy it. You're as wet as a little puppy... Come now, own up to it."

"I... I... I do like it. Yes... It's good." Her voice was wavering with a sensual shrill.

"My little pup, pup, pup." Her uncle whispered in her ear and then pushed up into the heart of her bowels and laughed heartily as though a victory had been won.

Linda moaned with the new onslaught of pleasure that filled her body. This time she felt that she was on the verge of having an huge orgasm. Stimulated and primed, she wished to carry the fuck to its ultimate glory. She took the man's testicles and adeptly toyed with them. She even pulled on them, indicating that he should not spare the rod to spoil the child. Linda wanted him deep, very deep within her.

Arthur was getting his just rewards now. He reeled with the throbbing sensation of pre-orgasmic pleasure, roaring with joy and impulsively biting into Linda's back as he hammered away in her asshole with his huge prick.

Linda felt her orgasm creeping up bit by bit, and then, to strengthen her own climax, Arthur unleashed his spunk in three mighty spasms, flooding her seething rectum. The young girl shook and hissed with pleasure as white streams of come poured down over her cunt-lips, dousing the expensive divan. Her guts were wounded, but her body had ascended to an unknown paradise.

Despite the ejaculation Arthur's cock stood rigid, as though it refused to acknowledge its diminishing powers. It remained lodged in Linda's anus as though it wanted to ride forever in that new tunnel of love.

Arthur was proud of his performance. He had far surpassed his brazen nephew. He withdrew his cock, dripping with sperm and wet shit, and placed it under the nose of his still-trembling niece. It was covered with a mixture of white, yellow and brown slime.

"Look at it Linda. Isn't it magnificent, covered with the shit of your asshole?"

Linda didn't answer, but she took a chance and fondled the semi-stiff member.

"Now, chicken dumpling, you're going to suck on it

properly and clean if off. You're quite capable of doing such a thing with that pretty mouth of yours, aren't you?"

Linda was in such a feverish sensual state that she simply couldn't refuse such a request. She took the phallus by the root and shoved it between her lips. She lapped and licked and sucked, and uncle Arthur was enraptured by the marvellous job she did. After a certain time, she felt it become hard again. Of course, this excited her all the more. She even felt disposed to renew the love session, any way uncle Arthur wished to suggest. But Arthur pushed her away. It wasn't a vicious push, it was gentle and he smiled at the young apprentice.

"Take it easy. You're going to swallow me alive! I can see that down deep you're a real glutton for this type of sausage. You're even more famished than your sister Brigette."

Linda looked at her uncle in great astonishment. She knew Brigette had spent a good part of her summer vacation at the villa. She had hardly seen her sister, who was a year older than she and was enroled in another college. Linda didn't have a chance to talk to her and find out what happened at the villa. It would have been helpful if she was warned in advance.

"You mean that with Brigette... it happened as well?"

Linda lay still, breathing deeply. Arthur put his hand on her breast.

"Just telling that story makes me excited. I think that I'm ready to make love again."

Arthur fell into the saddle without any trouble. Linda was lying back spread-eagled on the divan, wet and waiting. Apparently the story had made its effects on her as well.

"You're sure you don't want me to take you by the anus, first of all?"

Linda looked up at him and then lowered her eyes, showing him that she was his humble servant.

"Later on," she murmured softly, her eyes still glancing at the floor. "It still hurts... I would like to try... the other way first."

"Alright then. Open your legs up wide." Arthur's hands rubbed up and down the young body, moulding its form.

The young lass opened her legs as far as they could go and Arthur aimed his great prick at her dripping cunt.

"Now be careful, because this time you're going to feel it.

I mean business. Prepare yourself."

And in one slip of his magic wand he was in her, snug and warm. Linda had the odd sensation that she was being devirginized a second time. She felt she was being invaded for good now, and with a cock worthy of mention. The neophyte was performing a real task this time. She tasted the hardened cock as it pressed to the very depths of her cunt. She thought, she cried, she moved to and fro and caught the rhythm of the staunch piston that powered into her with all its might.

She even took Arthur by his hips and made him abide to a movement that was closer to what she liked. Finally they synchronized their pace and were soon in perfect bliss, building and building to the supreme moment.

Linda reflected on how good it was. She pinched Arthur's rump and with another hand she squeezed his balls and the base of his cock and it throbbed like a huge muscle, which it most certainly was, raw and alive with animal force.

Her uncle mounted her brutally. His weight crushed her and he beat her with his feverish body. Arthur's stomach pushed against her young lower belly with all the force of tidal wave. But Linda, pushed backward on the divan to the point where her head dropped off the edge, didn't mind the attack one bit. The girl ate it up. She had wild thoughts about a bull, a sturdy bull raping her.

"My strong, wonderful bull." These words issued from her lips and she couldn't prevent herself from muttering them several times.

"That's right. I'm a bull and you're a young calf. Why not?" Uncle Arthur bucked like one and renewed his thrusts to a punishing intensity.

Linda moaned and groaned without stopping. She no longer had to concentrate on her pleasure. Pleasure had consumed her and it was igniting holy fires within. She came almost without realizing it and her cunt juice cascaded between her shapely thighs.

"Oh, how good it is... It's so good..." She cried for the third time as a stronger orgasm gripped her loins, forcing her to tremble and shudder like a tree in a windstorm.

She felt her uncle's hot sperm shooting into her, and the two brought their respective orgasms to a wild, mutual climax.

Uncle and niece had harmonized well in their act of love –

a brutal, ardent love that was only to be the beginning.

They moved around a bit. It was the aftermath and the languor of the immense passion that had stirred them. Then, tired and limp, the two buckled in silence. Linda could no longer move her arm. The calf had lost its footing.

"I'm dead," she uttered briefly.

Uncle Arthur didn't say a thing.

♦

Arthur lay there thinking of a future treatment to administer on his lovely young niece.

Until then, they had just made love. How boring it was for him. He was a real connoisseur and, above all, he was gifted with a superb imagination. It was his duty to take care of the girl and initiate her into the realms of love in the best tradition of the family.

He moved away from the girl and went to his desk. As the light darkened in his library, he brightened his table lamp and began to write a few words.

...I find that the younger they are the more susceptible they are to ruthless attacks. Since their imaginations are wildly alive, they combine the little experience they have had thus in their lives and apply it to the act. The act is briskly approved when it suggests the erotic and the implausible for them. Strange creatures, everyone. For Brigette, it was a horse, for she never forgot the huge equestrian animal's cock, hard and ready to function on the female who was grazing in the next pasture. For Linda, the bull. She was looking for the barrel-chested fellow who could snort and prove his valour against the odds of the sword... and then there was blood in her mind, signifying the deflowering...

Everything was clear in his writer's head. He pulled out a cigarette and casually lit it as he slumped back into his leather armchair.

A few circles of misty smoke helped him to tint the air around him and clear his thoughts. He hunched over his documents and read.

...The young 12-18 are ~~essentially~~ romantic. Reality eludes them and they have no intention coming to grips with this unpleasant monster. Reality is a spanking, a chiding, harsh words.

Reality, for them, is morality, adult society, and the humdrum of social this and social that...

Later on he read a passage that made him take notice, and a smile curled his lips.

...Teach your child, father, teach him a good dose of it. There's the hairbrush, your belt. Don't use a newspaper, it's too weak. Mix the blood in that child of yours and give him some hope for the future. Let his romanticism win over all in the final run, but first let him taste the sweet brutality of pain. Break his britches, or more delightfully, concentrate on your daughter, daddy dear. And if you don't have one, go adopt one quickly or you'll go mad. You're getting on and so is your mistress, perfumed and dry, trying so hard to be the flower she was and never will be again.

Punishment to evoke pleasure. Look into it.

It's worth a try. (Consult list of punishing devices in Vol. 13, pages 164–246.) Punishment, pugilism, power, precision, perseverance, plunder, positivism, pleasure, pulsations, probing, pleasure and pure pleasure. Is there any doubt that "P" – yes, standing for prick, pornography, and pimp – is my favourite letter...?

Arthur closed his book and crushed out his cigarette. He went over to the cabinet at the end of the room and unlocked it. He appeared to be checking its contents. After a swift glance, he closed it.

He tip-toed over to the girl, who was laying there crumpled and worn, and with his forefinger he traced a "P" ever so lightly on her bare back.

chapter three

When Linda opened her eyes, she discovered the pitch darkness of night. She caught sight of her uncle standing not too far away. Arthur had taken two glasses and a bottle from his private cabinet. He held out one of the receptacles half-filled with whiskey.

"Here, drink this. It will do you good."

"But, but – I don't drink," Linda protested. Her uncle seemed irritated and the two thin lines on his forehead furrowed with vexation.

"Now don't be silly. Drink it."

The young girl used her better judgement and did as she was told. Although she made horrible faces and the liquid truly burned her throat, she managed to swallow it all the same. In all her young virginal life it was the first time she had tasted hard liquor.

"Now it's my turn to drink."

He took his glass and approached Linda's cunt with a very serious expression on his face. Then he poured the liquid into her belly-button. With hungry lips he followed the alcohol as it ran down to her pubic triangle. Once more he poured the liquor and this time it rolled down her thighs. Rapaciously he drank from the roiling fountain. Linda hurled her painful cries. The alcohol was burning her tender sex. Arthur buried his thin, elegant head between her immaculate thighs. Above, he let drip the last drops of whiskey onto her curly bush and then slobbered away like a thirsty madman.

Linda soon felt less pain, due to the expert licking manoeuvres of her highly-skilled uncle. She offered her pussy without any precaution, happy to be attacked by this ardent flow of affection. His tongue searched and searched as though it were looking for a maraschino cherry. While his face plunged deep within her aching cunt lips, his other hand found the whiskey bottle. Without the slightest hesitation or further ado, Arthur aimed the neck of Haig and Haig at the girl's sopping anus. It plugged in with a slurping noise that shocked and embarrassed Linda. With a brusque effort he flipped the helpless lass over in the air and began to pour the whiskey down her entrails in a burning enema. Linda squealed her pain and fright, which were equally acute. The sudden flood of liquid, a powerful burning liquid at that, caused an eruption of suffering in the vicinity of the girl's over-heated sex. At last an uncorking sound came from the adolescent's rear, indicating that the bottle had made its exit as violently as it had entered.

Immediately, Arthur's head was there to replace the glass cock. He loved alcohol and adored sex, and he was a man who loved to have his cake and eat it at the same time. Arthur disdained the misuse of pleasures. He was proud of his delicate gourmet tendencies, and he gave a royal proof of his aristocracy and a rough account of his virility.

Linda's little snatch turned brown as she scratched her blistered anus. She whimpered and moaned as she prepared to voyage on the turbulent road of further erotic indecencies.

"The best of scotch mixed with the excrement of my fair niece Linda," Arthur howled with personal triumph, and his laughter was shrill and piercing. "What could be better than this wholesome aperitif? Haven't you ever been buttfucked by a bottle of whiskey before, my dear? Think what you've missed."

Totally mortified, Linda could not and would not respond to such an impossible question. Her uncle appeared to be completely drunk with his sense of power and amusement.

She thought of getting up and going to the toilet, but the eager fingers of her probing uncle forbade her to move. Suddenly she let go with a stream of scalding urine, which splashed mercilessly into Arthur's handsome face. Linda tried in vain to hold back, but the pressure on her bladder was too strong. Thus she squirted a yellow flow of steaming piss flush on her uncle's mouth.

But Arthur did not quit his post. He was inextinguishable. He gulped down the steaming fluid greedily, smacking his lips. Ready to receive the last discharge from either orifice, and already covered with shit and urine, Arthur created such an impression on the Linda's sensitive temperament that the poor girl turned half-way around and vomited.

Almost in a faint from the repulsive sight she had been witness to, Linda did not see her uncle scamper to the chair in which he placed his clothes.

Arthur slipped a leather belt from his trousers as he clinched his teeth. Briskly he hovered over Linda before unleashing a wicked blow which slithered off the girl's lovely back. She was so surprised that she held back the cry that hung quivering on her lips.

Once again Arthur's hand circled in the air and a second stroke came crashing down with such tremendous force that a red mark was tattooed immediately on the girl's pale shoulders.

This time Linda howled with pain and her body trembled with fear. She had expected the worse and it might have been terrible, but it all came whistling down with the third thundering swipe of the leather strap.

Linda rolled on the carpet, partly to ward off the pain and partly to escape the furious blows. But her uncle, who had not the slightest intention of letting up, reigned supreme dictator of his young captive. He aimed at her pale buttocks next, and a grid of livid marks was thatched there in the space of a few minutes. From there he worked upward to her breasts.

The young kitten jumped in the air, grovelled on the floor and desperately tried to hide under the table. Her twists and turns had one singular effect on Arthur – they excited him all the more. He redoubled his punishment under the stupefied gaze of the writhing, zebra-marked Linda.

"You little bitch. You'll have enough to be thirsty with. I'll skin you, my pet." He puffed and blustered his threats.

"Please, no more... Enough, enough!" Linda felt that she had *already* been skinned.

Then, from her anus, a dark substance flowed out. It wasn't her fault. The sudden emotion and fright, not to mention the enema of malt, had given her the 'shits'. Her brown, bubbling faecal matter soiled the carpet and the room was quickly filled with a nauseating odour of urine and excrement, mixed with fresh sweat and traces of come.

"I should saw you in half, my little animal beauty. What would you say if I made you eat all that? Aren't you ashamed – dirtying the carpet that way?" Arthur didn't quit his lashing one iota, even as he lectured the beaten captive.

Linda hung her head. At that exact moment and in that woeful condition she would have accepted anything. She no longer had any will and her sensations were a mass of confusion. She could not endure the punishment and yet, despite herself, she was now realizing violent orgasms provoked by the rapid belt-lashes her sadistic uncle was firing between her legs, the tip of the belt snaking in and out of her gaping pussy. What *was* she to believe, in her shell-shocked state?

Her uncle finally ceased his whipping. He glowered at the humbled torso spattered with red, blue and black marks. Arthur watched the broken body creep toward him on all fours. He stood motionless as a tombstone, gazing upon the crushed creature who was now hugging and kissing his legs.

The greying man felt his cock grow hard again, and the lively head of his niece ventured instinctively to the throbbing glans. She gobbled him into her hot mouth, sucking the erection like a child with a lollipop.

Uncle Arthur let the girl have her fun for awhile, but he had other intentions. He soon pushed the drunken youngster away, and addressed her in an a voice full of unbending authority.

"Come – we are going to take a bath together."

He made her get up and after crossing the large study, he opened a door, almost hidden from view. Arthur led his niece into a bathroom which was large and tiled in rose squares. The bathroom not only contained a large bathtub, but an equally large divan which was covered by a white drapery. There were other accessories in the bathroom and Linda gazed with horror at the medicine chest.

She closed her eyes and her mind drifted into the realms of wild imagination. Was she entering the domain of paradise or hell? "I'll prepare the bath." Arthur took little time to turn on the bathtub faucets.

Linda took a look around and found the object of her sudden desire. She reeled over to the toilet and straddled it without the least consideration of Arthur's presence. She farted and turned red as gouts of come, whiskey and shit spattered the bowl. Arthur smiled and his lips curved in contentment.

"Why you look very lovely in that position," he leered.

He tiptoed over to the sitting waif and presented her with his stiff prick. Linda, still straddling the toilet seat, took the cock between her teeth avidly. She felt two pleasures at once. At the same time as she was shitting, she had a full-blown, plunging cock down her throat.

In her wildest imagination she would never have dreamed all this was possible. It was only that morning that she had arrived, pure and innocent, just to spend a vacation by the sea. Never in her most daring fantasies would she have concocted these wild scenes and perverted sensations. And yet, reality had already soared beyond the most powerful hallucination.

Arthur, who was admiring the situation with the eye of a true libertine, licked his lips at each plop of wet shit that issued from the girl's angelic asshole.

"Stop. I don't want to come right now, since I have other pleasures in view."

Linda, who had finished her needs, leaned over to grab the toilet paper, but Arthur's hand stopped her from exercising any further action. Neatly he unravelled the roll of paper and wiped the insides of her buttocks clean himself. Then he bent over and carefully, fastidiously licked out his niece's pink and brown anus. Enraptured, she pushed back against his probing tongue until her sphincter was clamped around its tip, trying to milk his come into her burning rectum. For a while he let her impale herself in that way, then he withdrew.

"Come here, the bath is ready." Arthur led naked Linda by the hand.

They stepped into the over-sized bath at the same time. The water came up to their hips. Linda felt a prickly sensation caused by the tepid water, which soothed and burned her skin at the same time. She had recently been soundly thrashed and she was highly sensitive from head to toe. Little by little she became used to the warming effect of the water as she watched her uncle soap himself vigorously.

Then Arthur soaped his niece as though he were washing a puppy-dog, the stinging lather infesting the criss-cross slashes across her skin. Linda made faces and it was obvious that her wounds gave her much distress.

"Now, now..." Her uncle's voice grew paternal and

debonair. "You're as dirty as a pigling and you squeal at a piece of soap. If you don't behave, I shall have to punish you – and you can just guess how I'll go about it." He meant business and Linda had no doubts about it. She didn't have to strain her imagination any more. Linda had been initiated and she now knew anything could happen. This bathroom scene was a far cry from being dispensed with. Surprises were undoubtedly in store for her. And, what was most surprising of all, she found herself welcoming the unexpected, the unknown with an almost voracious pleasure.

Her uncle stood up in the bathtub and spread the soap all over her fine body. She was soon covered with soap suds, particularly her fuzzy bush. Linda thought of the many times she had accomplished this same act with just a hint of the pleasure it might give if treated by some worthy hands. Reality supersedes fiction, and her uncle's hand spread her thighs in an effort to thoroughly soap her ass, belly and inner thighs. A delicate finger wiggled in her anus. Linda was careful to conceal her pleasure. She wriggled with satisfaction.

"Now we're going to buttfuck in a bathtub, my dear. Hang on to the railing and spread apart, darling mermaid."

Linda didn't have to be coaxed twice. She felt a small tidal wave encircle her pussy and the rippling sensation meant that a flesh torpedo was being well aimed at her foaming nether regions.

A direct hit. The penis slipped into her hungry rim like an oiled fist into a waiting glove, burying itself to the hilt. Meanwhile, Linda's cunt was being washed out by the warm soapy suds which welled with each thrust of Arthur's loins.

This time the young girl squirmed and squealed with pleasure. Never before had she felt the true value of her uncle's prick. It went in and out with all the relentless power of a piston. When she turned her head, she saw the foam floating on the water's surface, the turbulence of their two sexes in heated collision. She couldn't help gazing back at Arthur's face. He appeared transfigured as he took on the aspects of a demon and an angel all at once.

"It's magnificent. You're wonderful." Linda was sincere in her praise, though she suffered a bit due to the width of Arthur's cock. It was difficult to withstand his huge erection in her small asshole, and it was with both pain and pleasure that she soaked the erotic stimulation of this most novel bathtime adventure.

chapter four

The time had come for Linda and her uncle to withdraw from their soap-sud game. But they splashed with pleasure like two fiery animals at the climax, and a thick white substance, streaked with red and brown, floated gelatinously on the surface of the water.

Arthur was the first to scamper out of the tub. He took a large beach towel and rubbed himself dry as his niece bounced out of the bath dripping from head to foot. Playfully Arthur lashed out with a flick of the towel. The sting caught Linda right between her buttocks. The girl howled and tried to dodge a second whack that slithered off her thighs.

The helpless lass ducked behind the toilet stool for protection. And this is where she had made her mistake. Arthur smiled cruelly, and it was all too apparent that he had found a new method of entertaining himself. A wicked strike of the towel, cradling around the toilet lever, flushed the bowl and gave the girl a start.

Linda ran from her hiding place and found herself cornered along the tiled walls. Arthur tracked her down like a favourite hunt. The towel, partially wet, hummed in the air and caught the adolescent across the breasts.

"Please, dear uncle, no more." Linda had uttered the words that could only stimulated her enraged relative further.

"Here's some 'no more' for you, my sweet." His teeth glittered.

Several blows buckled Linda to her knees as she cringed in horror. What made matters worse was the wet skin, lashed by the heavy soaking towel. This caused red eruptions about her lower abdomen, breasts and nipples.

Arthur's penis grew large yet again, and it vibrated in the steamy pungent mist of the bathroom. The haze, combined of heat, sweat and humidity, hampered the ardent uncle in his task of taming a young vixen.

Furiously he threw the towel aside and dragged the limp girl to the shower. There, under the rain of the sprinkler, uncle Arthur buttfucked his lovely niece while standing. Catching her flush in the asshole, he tweaked the tips of her wet nipples with his dexterous fingers.

The immense flood of ever-changing thrills, mixed with the delights of orgasm, swept through Linda's body and her heart beat like a trip hammer. It was strange how pain, a pain which she felt she could never endure, turned into a magnificent treat whenever Arthur's cock plunged so deep within her. The man already loved to piston in and out of her cunt, and now that her asshole had also been broken in, a new level of voluptuous pleasure possessed her being.

Their movements were even more frenetic than the downpour of water. Linda's bottom moved rhythmically forward and back while Arthur cupped her breasts and tickled her rigid nipples. Both of them, inflamed by the wonderful pressure and temperature of the water, performed like animals. Their moans and panting sounds were drowned out by the flooding shower, but when they finally climaxed an echo of ecstasy burst in the cell of the bathroom, crackling against the tiles.

Arthur, as capricious as ever, was the first to leave the shower stall. Evidently he was a master of his own acts, and was decisive in all his movements. He quickly closed the glass door on Linda, who naturally hollered to be let out. When she turned off the shower, she shivered and when she kept it running, the water temperature mounted at an alarming rate.

Arthur had a strange way of amusing himself. Luckily for Linda, Alice suddenly knocked on the door and asked for her uncle.

"What do you want? Go away." Arthur was indignant.

"You wanted me to wear that special outfit with the black tights and red bra." Her voice cooed with honey.

Arthur returned to the very pleasant reality of his present situation. It was true that he had summoned Alice for an encounter at six. She was as malleable as a child. For quite awhile, he had enjoyed a rare amusement with Alice and he was not going to be denied of his pleasure because of a wet niece.

He bundled himself up in his bath-robe and scurried out of the bathroom. Linda was free and relieved, although she at once felt betrayed and alone. It was the first time she had ever sensed the pangs of jealousy.

Curiosity mixed with lust guided her to the room in which Arthur and Alice were ready to entangle voluptuously.

Naturally it would take place in the library. Arthur negligently – or perhaps it was on purpose – left the door open. Linda had a perfect spot from where to take in the performance of the two professionals.

Alice was standing semi-naked in a pair of very high-heeled shoes. They were bright orange and gave her legs, which were sheathed in black lace stockings, a superb silhouette. The maid, who had seemed so insignificant before, was bewitching in her extravagant costume.

One of the odd accoutrements of the outlandish outfit was her red bra. She appeared uncomfortable with it, and she squirmed painfully when she had to make the slightest effort with her upper body.

The maid's face was painted up like that of a low-grade prostitute. Her lips and eye make-up were terribly exaggerated and her face was an invitation to new levels of licentiousness.

Arthur registered his approval. A snide smile crept across his handsome face as he squeezed Alice's two ripe breasts. The curvy maid let out a yell that pierced Linda's ear-drums. For a moment Linda imagined that Alice was having her period, but then she reasoned that it was something else, something that was on the inside lining of the bra. Later on, she found that she was perfectly right in her reasoning. Sharp little needle points caused the torture and humiliation of the unwholesome garment.

"Don't cry like that. You'll draw everyone's attention." Arthur was displeased with Alice and his hand pressed the girl's cheeks in a sign of admonishment.

Then the elegant man tugged down the young lady's panties and plunged his face into the grove of her pubic hair. The perfume of her pussy was so strong that it caught the nostrils of the peeking Linda. The smell was nauseating. It reeked so pungently of unwashed come and cheap perfume that Linda held her nose for a few minutes. She was astonished at how her uncle was able to bear such a repulsive stench.

Meanwhile Arthur's mouth had gone unerringly to the very heart of the maid's steaming pussy. Alice's legs drifted wider and wider apart as she gripped Arthur's damp hair. Her knees began to shake as her lover gave his all. Linda remembered how superb Arthur was a pussy-licking, and she knew that Alice was having a riotously good time of it. Her legs and buttocks looked divine, raised high and spread open with the orange high heels raking at the ceiling, her lascivious posture due to the encouragement of Arthur's skilful tongue.

A whimsical moan trickled from Alice's throat, and Linda felt her own cunt becoming wetter and wetter as her youthful eyes drank in the delicious scene.

Her uncle's hands wandered up to the spiked bra and his two large palms squeezed the maid's tits. Alice turned faint and she bit her lower lip, drawing blood.

Yet she didn't complain. If she did, she knew she would receive nothing but painful abuse. She was shaken by pleasure, but at the same time she was forced to abide the suffering administered by her noble lover's hands.

Alice's fingernails clawed in Arthur's hair as she tried to relieve the metal massage on her breasts. The uncle, steady at his post, lapped away at her pussy and continued to abuse her tits.

The bitter and the sweet were combined as Alice ground her hips. She did not know whether to seek a haven of rest by pushing the man away, or enjoy the paradisiacal pleasures to be earned by sticking it out.

Thus Arthur controlled his victim – or loved one, depending on the point of view one wishes to take.

Linda later found out that Arthur had theories on sex that were declared 'revelational and astounding' by experts in the field. Arthur's books were not known publicly but they had a secret audience that cherished them far above the classics.

Well, at the moment the great sexologist was performing his deeds on a paltry maid. He could have had the pick of metropolitan women, but he had his reasons. Arthur knew how to discriminate and above all he knew what he wanted. Alice filled the menu, and he was satisfied with his choice.

As the youngster reeled in a pathetic scene of torture and

delight, Arthur slipped away and plucked a rubber dildo from his drawer. Swiftly he flew back to his purring cat, replaced his mouth in her bush and licked her out as before. Then, deftly, he plugged the dildo into the small opening of Alice's asshole. Linda was amazed to see how everything was regulated and planned.

Arthur pumped away with the instrument while his tongue ripped in and out of the maid's soaking vagina. Alice's eyes turned in her head like a slot machine. Slowly they came out cherry red and Linda knew Arthur was closing in on the jackpot.

With one great cry Alice unburdened her immense orgasm in the gentleman's mouth. He sucked her dry, drinking down torrents of hot thick cunt-juice, as he controlled his erection in order to keep from ejaculating.

The thunder of Alice's inarticulate moans excited Arthur, and he violently ripped away her panties. Brutally he slammed his swollen cock into the maid's cunt, while he continued to manipulate the false phallus which was reaming out her slippery asshole with amazing dexterity.

For a while, the two ground away in a deep vacant frenzy. They were like two violent dancers who were given to shaking voluptuously to their own inner rhythms in the centre of a grand ballroom, only this was Arthur's library, and the scene was intimate and warm.

Linda was inflamed by the expert movements of the two superb lovers, who were by now glowing in ecstasy. She began to masturbate, heaving with lust. Her middle finger went all the way up her cunt as her tongue fell out of her mouth. Saliva dripped from her lips, while a sticky substance trickled on the carpet from her dripping snatch. She had made up her mind to live vicariously with the two lovers. A secret desire gripped her, and she felt an intense need to bite into Alice's rump.

But she didn't dare, fearing the punishment, which would be perhaps...

Her thought was broken like a twig at the sound of Arthur's muffled voice.

"Linda – come here and join us."

Dear Arthur could not have given her a more pleasing present.

She was on the spot in no time. And Linda performed her

functions like a trouper. With her teeth she pulled out the rubber dildo from Alice's asshole, and put her head straight between her butt-cheeks without even demanding permission from her notorious uncle.

While Arthur laboured in and out of the maid's sticky bush, Linda deeply penetrated her asshole with her thin, thirsty tongue. Occasionally she licked at Arthur's tight balls, and the base of his red cock as it thrust in and out of Alice's cunt.

Arthur, who was no novice in the giving pleasure, now gave up Alice's pussy for a dip into Linda's hungry asshole.

The man was dripping with come, although he had not as yet reached the supreme moment. He hammered his cock into the half-inch opening, giving Linda such a violent thrill that she redoubled her anal licking and lapping, much to the delight of Alice who was in seventh heaven.

"Is everyone happy?" Arthur asked, partly in pride and partly with self-imposed rapture.

There was no response. The two young ladies were too busy reaping the harvest of their vast pleasure ride. Alice suddenly felt a wave of gratitude which she felt she should deliver to her master, who was pushing the girls into the wall with his pounding. She abandoned her position to kneel at Arthur's rear, and started to chew at his rump, running her tongue down until it slipped into the musky crevice of his rectum.

The trio thus changed two or three times, without any unfavourable change or let-down in sheer pleasure and ecstasy.

After twenty minutes of intense orgiastic couplings, the threesome unloaded their come into the mouth and bowels of their respective partners and then tumbled to the ground in a heap.

Arthur was the first to regain his footing, after wiping the sweat from his brow. He smiled ironically as he gazed at the two limp torsos wrapped together on the floor.

"Enough is enough ladies," he laughed jovially. "We'll be at it again another time. Don't you realize it's after eight and dinner isn't even prepared? What kind of a household do you think I'm running anyway? Alice, get to the kitchen before you receive treatment 3X!"

That was all the spent maid had to hear. She scurried out of the room pale with fright, clutching her garments. Linda was rocked out of her slumber by the sudden departure of the luscious maid.

Arthur helped his niece to her feet. The first thing Linda did was to throw her arms around her uncle's neck, but he quickly pushed her aside, showing that he hated the idea of over-sentimentality.

"Now go and see what Robert and that tigress are up to. I have my ideas on the subject. Tell them to come down for dinner immediately after they've showered, I'm sure they'll need to be refreshed after their work-out."

He walked over to his niece and affectionately placed his hand under her chin. His handsome gaze met her large wet eyes and he looked deep within, as through trying to decode the secrets of her adolescent soul.

"Are you happy here, Linda?" He wanted the truth, and he was not going to settle for anything else.

"Oh, uncle... I don't know. I think so. You see, I never, never..."

He walked to his desk and picked up her words as though he had known them for a long while. "...Never expected to see the likes of it."

He tapped a cigarette on the back of his hand and his eyes suddenly changed. Linda detected a shade of grey darken in the sombre sockets.

"You'll find, Linda dear, that we have only just began to know each other. I promise you that a full-dressed adventure lies in front of you. So far we have just engaged in penny-ante affairs. Just wait, and you'll be astonished the more."

With these words, Arthur opened the door and Linda knew that she was to go and call his mistress and Robert. A flood of broken ideas crept through her mind like the quick fall of a spring.

She was lucid and careful to select the true value of the sudden inspiration that throbbed in her veins and heart.

All at once she turned beet-red. She felt ashamed, haunted by her acts. Linda knew that they would live with her a long while. She had been robbed of her innocence. *But what of it,* she thought. Her puritanism had always been a bother. It was better to be done with it once and for all.

Then on the other hand? No... There was no doubt about

it – she came from a sensual, lustful family. There was no sense refuting hereditary. She was a member of Arthur's clan and she decided to be proud of it. However, she knew she was unlike Arthur. So much different than her uncle, that a sudden terrifying fear gripped her heart.

She climbed the stairs feverishly. Linda had an errand to perform and she made a noble effort to erase her morbid thoughts. At the end of the hall she tapped lightly on Robert's door. There was no answer. She heard a blend of strained voices. Linda opened the door and was not at all surprised to see Robert and Lola enlaced like two serpents.

"Fuck me in the rear, Robert honey. Do it good, you young whipper-snapper – or I'll bite off your cock."

Lola playfully nibbled on the boy's ear-lobe. Their bodies oozed sweat and an odour that was purely sensual and pungent. Linda didn't have the courage to intrude, and yet she had a mission to perform.

"Dinner will be ready soon. Uncle Arthur sent me to tell you to wash up."

She looked guiltily at the couple as though she were a real kill-joy, destined to spoil their fun. It was apparent that they dismissed her words disdainfully. Linda found that her throat was dry and she could not utter the same words for a second time.

Although she felt like running from the room, she was glued to the spot. Suddenly she became enthraled by Lola's seductively bouncing breasts. Robert had her from behind, and was jarring her with rapid plunges in the rear. Lola bucked forward with her hair wildly covering her handsome face.

Linda watched her heavy tits jiggle in the air. A burning urge to devour them incensed the girl, and in no time at all she found herself already kneeling on the bed sucking tenderly on the dark red nipples. Lola caressed Linda's head and she whispered in her ear stimulating words of love, her tongue caressing Linda's ear-lobe.

"Love them, my buttercup. Suck them well and nip on them as though they were ripe cherries. I'll make you queen, my dear. Take bigger mouthfuls, Linda darling. Come now, you've grown up my little one."

Robert had buried his throbbing cock in Lola's sweaty,

voluptuous asshole. Through sheer determination he kept back his orgasm as he bit into the neck of the lovely brown-skinned beauty.

Linda no longer knew why she had come into their secret abode, but she relinquished all questions as she sank into the abandon of lust. Lola's breasts were so juicy and delicious that the girl felt she could suck on them forever.

Lola sweetly fingered Linda's pussy, and she knew every sensitive crease and fold of a young girl's cunt. Her long fingers caused a hot saliva to run from Linda's mouth. The trio pitched deliriously and the be springs squealed with the burden of their love-making.

None of them had eaten for hours. They were all healthy and gifted with enormous appetites, but they had long forgotten dinner time. In their games of love, their concentration was on the fruits of passion and nothing else.

A sheet of condensation covered the windows as the three bodies smouldered with caresses and tonguings. Robert became purple with his tremendous effort to sustain his drive.

Linda and Lola certainly wanted the encounter to continue until doomsday. For the first time they had found out the real capacities of one another. Delighted to find that they were in perfect harmony, the two females bestowed their respective affections and art upon each other.

Then with a gust of wind the door flew open and uncle Arthur stormed in, as angry as a lion. Linda looked askance at the enraged man without letting a teat slip out of her mouth. Arthur's eyes turned violently red.

"So this is what you're all up to. Linda disobeys me first of all, and then of course Robert and my fair lady persuaded her to join them. Well it needs a lesson, this perverted act does."

Arthur brandished a whip that shook between his legs. Words flew hot and heavy.

"Lola you are a no-good bitch. I hold you responsible for the deviations of these children. Robert, if you continue to be as presumptions and aggressive in your manner, there will be no more use of the car and I promise you that I'll put that great cock of yours in a sling. Linda, disobedience costs dearly in my household and I will not allow it for a minute. You'll learn your lesson very shortly, my dear niece."

With quick sharp strides he came to the bed and hovered over the trio as if momentarily paralysed. Then his lithe frame went into action as his arm furiously wielded the lash.

A first punishing stroke whammed across Robert's back, driving his cock more securely into the sucking hole of mistress Lola's ass. A second blow encircled the threesome, who were literally moulded together by its force. It caught Linda on the buttocks and thighs and she winced, biting into Lola's poor breasts. The tigress howled as she felt the sudden teeth stab into her flesh.

Blow after blow rained down on the naughty trio. Arthur was truly mad and he intended to have everyone pay for her and his misdeeds.

Robert pleaded for him to let up, but Lola had a strange contorted look on her face. She was a victim of mixed emotions, and Linda was disturbed and astonished to see a whole range of facial expressions emanate from her lovely, sensual friend.

The whipping had achieved an opposite effect on Lola. She was writhing with a sickly sensual pleasure that would not diminish.

Her excitation became unbearable, and it produced an odd effect on Linda and Robert. The two youngsters weathered the storm of the whip and they too took refuge in a newly arisen pleasure. They scrambled together like hungry startled animals. Their sexes were wet and their mouths were bubbling with saliva as they renewed their orgy baptised in blood.

"Have it out, you three. Get it all out of your system. Tomorrow is another day and we will see what comes out of your misbehaviour. But you'll bear the marks of today's chastisement. Take that... and that... for your pleasure!"

Arthur was livid with rage. He refused to believe that his law and order had backfired in such a way. Lola had known the exceptional man too long, and she had stayed with him for very personal reasons. She knew how to come out on top even with an intelligent fox like Arthur.

Robert was the first to let loose and have a shattering orgasm. His prick spasmed in the Lola's majestic asshole as his balls emptied every last drop of semen into her bowels. He withdrew with a wet plop. A small trickle of whitish spunk clung to the crack of her ass, mixing with a brownish colour that emitted a bittersweet stench. The odour filled the room and not one of the four complained about it. They revelled in its musky allure, and Linda, driven wild, was the second to burst wide open, her cunt-juices showering everybody. She captured Lola in her arms and her mouth slipped from the breasts down to the belly button and then still lower to the gaping cunt. She buried her face in the rosy folds, tonguing away with youthful fire.

Arthur gave his whip up for lost. He was curiously taken by the mass of feverish flesh. Now he would teach them a lesson. Within warning, the elegant master plunged his stout cock into the dry asshole of his nephew, who bellowed in agony and seemed thunderstruck at this unprecedented onslaught.

"There, my dear Robert – a sudden surprise for your manhood. No-one ever told you that a rear end is a haven not to be denied, whether it is that of a young lady or a young gentleman. Don't look so pained, my dear fellow. You'll come out of it alright. You're a wee bit tight of course, but that will be straightened out in due time."

Robert fled with blood pouring from his anus, crushed by the humiliating experience.

At dinner that night he was unable to raise his head and respond to the jibes of his uncle. Lola though admitted she had come several times. And when asked how many, she timidly lowered her eyes and calculated...

"Four."

Linda knew that they were big, exorbitant ones. She had witnessed at least two monstrous monsoons that Lola blew out of her womb.

When Arthur turned toward Linda with his usual calm grace, he didn't have to wait long for the answer.

"Three."

Linda turned red and she attempted to cover her blushes with the whiteness of the napkin, which only served as a definite contrast.

"Then everybody is content. Well, let's dig into the chicken and eat heartily. Alice has also prepared a steak for each of us. We've got to regain the energy we lost in our foolhardy endeavours today."

It was difficult to say whether Arthur had a smile on his lips or whether they were contorted by the an unintentional memory of the whip's vicious bite.

"Alice, you may sit with us tonight. After all, you had a workout as well. Come in when you're ready my dear. I want us all to behave as one big happy family."

They all ate with gusto.

chapter five

At dinner, Arthur became pensive and his mind was working at double time. He tapped his fingers together and stroked his chin. Although he no longer seemed to have an appetite, his tablemates were eating rapaciously.

"I hope everyone finds the dinner as it should be? I made sure that it was carefully seasoned. Pepper and spices help in restoring amorous urges."

Arthur watched Linda snap the leg of the chicken and pick it up with her dainty fingers. She blushed as she noticed his prolonged stare. Little did she guess her uncle's thoughts. How he would have liked to pluck this young chicken apart for good.

Lola looked ravishing in her new blue gown, while Robert ate like a college football player. He kept filling his plate with potatoes and disgusted the refined Arthur, who looked at him with disdain.

Alice entered with a second plate of vegetables. She was dressed in a scanty outfit that was daring and extremely sexy. Her bosom jutted out pertly and her little bottom wiggled tightly under a strange looking pair of panties.

Suddenly Arthur snapped his fingers. He seemed to have had an idea that he rather relished.

"I would like to see you after dinner, Linda. It's for a matter... let's say a certain *dessert* that I have for you."

Linda looked surprised, and she slowly lost her appetite due to a growing perplexity. Arthur on the other hand, renewed his hunger and now ate almost as rapidly as Robert.

Lola rubbed her hand along Linda's knee, and the young adolescent felt a warm sensation creep between her thighs. Lola's hands were truly remarkable. The mere touch of this exceptional beauty had a stimulating effect on the young girl.

Their slight display of emotions dwindled as Arthur clapped his hands, signifying that he was wise to the pair's antics. When dinner was finally over, Arthur requested Linda to follow him into his library. She obeyed, docile and refined in her gracious steps.

Once in the library, Arthur gazed longingly at his niece. He fingered a book and turned a few pages, just to practice his touch. Arthur was a man of much nervous energy, and he had the habit of wringing his hands.

"Linda, I'm writing a story about a girl such as you. She's an unusual girl who represents adventure to the fullest extent. Her name is Ancella. I named her after an Egyptian princess who died a strange death at the early age of twenty-two. As the story goes, the young princess was walking in the nearby forest some few hundred yards from her castle, when she spied a bush sparsely covered with orange fruit. Her protectress, a woman of some seventy years of age, forbade her to taste the fruit. The princess became inquisitive and she tried some anyway, against the pleading of the elderly woman.

Three days later the princess was taken by a series of convulsions and she suddenly became terrifyingly lustful. Heretofore, she had been a virgin of the purest order, but suddenly this strange transformation fell upon her.

At first many of the court thought she had inherited the whorish instincts of her mother, a court concubine, but later they found she was truly a victim of a sexual passion and hunger that knew no bounds.

The girl literally raped every young and old servitor of the king and queen. It is said that she was soft-skinned and extremely beautiful, and her response to the male population was met with applause and pleasure. Disorder broke out in the kingdom and a veritable City of Sodom ensued."

Linda watched Arthur as he minutely described the many details of the fascinating story. The man's eyes glowed and he appeared to see the many sensual events before him as he told the tale.

"The princess died of sexual and sadistic abuse brought on mostly by her own hands. I have often wondered if the myth of the fruit is true, or whether it was her own nature that destroyed her. At any rate you can see that the story enthrals me. And what about you, doesn't it have its effect?"

Linda had no idea of how her uncle wanted her to answer, but she decided to adhere to his enthusiasm.

"It is an astounding story, if it is true?"

"What do you mean if it is true? I am convinced that it is. Why there is even some documentation attesting to its validity. I am really surprised, Linda, that you think that it is a mere figment of someone's imagination."

Linda was quick to ward off a possible burst of anger spell that she felt she might have to endure. Words were her best protection, although Arthur was rarely fooled by rhetoric or perfumed and flattering words.

"Oh, I'm sure it has some basis of truth in it. I was just wondering whether *all* of it can be substantiated."

Arthur smiled and his hands tightly grasped the book he was holding.

"Linda, you're a wonderful little liar in your way. But I must admit, I am fond of you."

They exchanged smiles. It was difficult to say whether it was an exchange between enemies or friends. Their expressions were tinged by a marked ambiguity.

"I only told you that story to let you know that you have become the princess Ancella for me. There is no fruit here to offer you, but everyday henceforth you will taste an exotic dish of fruit which I have ordered. They are all different, but I am sure one of them will have an effect on you."

He laughed crazily and at first Linda laughed with him, feeling that Arthur was giving vent to his peculiar sense of humour. Then it dawned on the youngster that he was quite serious in his endeavour.

A shiver caused Linda to grow pale and contemplate on her fate, on the defence she would have to present.

Words failed the girl and the only reaction she presented to her merciless uncle were a few drops of bitter tears.

"Enough of that. It is not going to help matters. I've made up my mind."

Linda appeared crushed, broken in two. Her uncle placed his sinewy arms around her shoulders. He kissed her hair and her temple and patted her on her rump.

"What do you think of Alice, my dear?"

Linda was shaken from her depression. It was a surprising question to hear after such a tense quarter of an hour.

"Why, she seems perfectly alright to me."

"Well, my little one, I've prepared a treat for you. You've had everyone amongst us with the exception of our delicious maid. It is only normal that you see for yourself what delicate, sensual delights she may have in store for you, and I hope the act will be a mutual affair."

Suddenly Linda's thoughts swiftly turned to Alice. She'd had a soupcon of the maid's asshole, and she was a luscious little thing alright. She was much more peppery and juicy than Lola. But there was something common in her that made Linda pout, despite her desire not to give her reactions away. However, if Alice was good enough for Robert, and even Arthur, then she must have *some* saving grace.

"You two young ladies are going to perform in front of me in just a few minutes. You know we have no cinema here or ballroom, and we have to make up our own entertainment."

Linda was led over to a sumptuous divan cover with a purple fabric that was warm and soft. Arthur told her that this was to be the decor of their love act.

He went over to his bureau and pressed a buzzer. It was obviously for Alice. Linda noticed that there were a series of buttons and that all Arthur had to do was press one or any given number and his 'victims' were requested to answer.

In no time flat, Alice entered the room. The maid was dressed in lace that was as scanty as the attire of a newly-wed. Her sexual commonness was exaggerated, but far from unpleasant. She looked like a tart, with her high heels and her split crotch panties and peephole bra.

On a closer glance, Linda was able to detect that oddity of attire which gave the girl a peculiar allure – although Alice could never have looked more sexual.

The girl wore frilly purple garters attached to old-fashioned black-brown stockings. Her extremely tight panties were chewed away, as if by moths. A swathe of pubic hair stuck out at one end, and a part of the curve of the left buttock made its appearance as well.

Alice had full breasts and they stood at attention in the jet black and white bra that scarcely covered their bulging orbs, the lipsticked nipples poking out. Extra height was gained through the use of very high Italian shoes, that blended with the ensemble.

For the first time in her sexual life, Linda desired to be a male. She had a strange desire for Alice, and she couldn't decide whether it was the clothing, or rather the lack of it, or whether it was Alice herself.

Uncle Arthur was quick to see that everything pointed toward success. He went over to his private cabinet and extracted an instrument Linda had never noticed before. The girl was awestruck when she saw a perfect replica of a man's penis made out of plastic or rubber (as far as she could make out) and attached to a belt. But it didn't take long for Linda to catch on to its use.

Arthur burst out in a winsome smile when Linda took the stiff rubber dick out of his hand and stepped into the strange harness as though she had made use of one all her life.

"You learn quickly, my princess. You'll soon see what it's like to be a male. I want you tell me your exact reactions. Please don't hide anything from me."

Cradling the false cock as though it were made of china, Linda aimed it at the frightened maid. The schoolgirl backed Alice to the couch and then stretched her out in a technique that made Arthur stroke his chin inquiringly.

With one knee Linda forced Alice's legs apart. With her long fingers she stripped the girl of her panties by merely ripping on the elastic. The material burst under her savage pull.

Alice was perplexed to see Linda delight in the role of masculine prowess. She even noticed the change in her eyes. The young adolescent gave positive proof of a male side of her nature.

Linda grabbed her cock, just as a proud lover would encircle the instrument he treasures. The girl tickled Alice's cunt lips with the head of the prick, before stabbing into the wet mass of hair.

One of Linda's hands cradled the buttocks of the voluptuous maid, tickling her glistening asshole and demonstrating that she was aware of the fine art bestowed by expert male lovers.

"Excellent, princess, excellent. I couldn't have done better myself." Arthur cheered her on, although his niece needed absolutely no encouragement whatsoever.

Very soon the dildo slid rigidly inside the depths of Alice's cunt. The young maid let out a moan of enjoyment. She hugged tightly to Linda's neck and even bit her lover on the ear-lobe. Arthur went behind his desk and began to take notes. His eyes wandered from the love scene back to the written page. He noticed the manoeuvres and dexterity of his lovely niece as she brought Alice to the dizzy heights of orgasm.

The maid began to drool, and her eyes seemed to go dead all at once. Linda was hungrily biting one of the youngster's tits while a hand wondered up and down her feverish vertebrae.

"I love that... Oh, oh... it's good, so good... love, love, love it."

Alice began a magnificent chant to her strange lover. She murmured little nothings in Linda's ear. Although the words were incoherent, they spurred Linda on.

The rubber cock gained a milky shine as it slipped in and out, in and out of Alice's soaking pussy. Alice was completely stretched open, and she gave her entire being to the passionate thrusts of the phallic bitch who was servicing her so adroitly.

Linda was panting away and although she showed signs of flagging, it was apparent that the whole scene excited her beyond belief.

The two girls, svelte and superb in their lesbian abandon, paraded their sexual depravity before the lecherous onlooker.

Linda could no longer control herself. She ripped off the garter belt and had the diminutive maid practically naked and devoid of her clothes. She pounded the synthetic cock into Alice's hole.

"Take her from behind," instructed Arthur, who was watching the scene while taking a flood of notes.

Linda did not have to be urged on. She pivoted the maid around and placed her dog-fashion on the divan. With one lusty plunge she managed to stick the enormous head of the dildo into her small but well-oiled anus. Alice groaned in pain, but she didn't protest to the sudden sodomization by her female partner.

A glossy sheen crept over Linda's forehead and it was evident that the girl was giving Alice her best. Linda's left hand was tickling her clit while her right was pinching and teasing her nipples.

Suddenly the two began to shudder and shake, and they screamed as they exploded in simultaneous orgasm, all their cunt juice spraying from their gushing pussies. A slow smear of brown trickled from Alice's anus. Alice was suffocating, crushed by the weight of Linda's hefty instrument. She had taken it from the front, and then succumbed to the terrible assault behind. But it felt so wonderful that she did not complain, indeed she pleaded for more pain, sweet pain such as only Linda was able to administer.

"Do it again. Please don't let up. I want it so badly. Again and again, darling!"

The two young kittens went at it with all their might. Linda did not spare her partner for one moment. After three more incredibly strong, consecutive orgasms, they both crumpled in a heap as if unconscious with ecstasy.

Arthur kept writing, and he failed to notice Linda's mouth creep slowly down Alice's body, her hot tongue lapping the sweat from her navel before plunging into the depths of her wide-open, come-covered pussy.

chapter six

Due to excessive fatigue, Arthur retired to his room early and left the others to their charming company.

Robert dozed off on the corner couch and when he awoke, he was not too surprised to see Linda and Lola interlaced in each other's arms. The young fellow threw his shoulders back and advanced toward the two women. An ironic smile dominated his features.

"Well, well, well. Aren't you going to invite me to your little get-together?"

Linda didn't know what to say, but Lola burst out in nervous laughter and exclaimed: "This young man is in need of something. Just look at him. He's holding us at gun point."

Needless to add that she was referring to Robert's cock, which stood at full attention, slightly twitching. He looked down at his proud tool like a hungry wolf and then his eyes wandered over the two nudes twined in their lewd coupling.

"What do you say, Linda? Shall we try his wares and see what he's worth?"

Robert didn't wait for an nod from either side. He approached the two and gave Lola's full thigh a slap with his left hand, Linda's marvellous breasts with his right.

"You'll see, my 'belles femmes'," he boasted. "Now to begin *there...*"

He jumped behind Lola and placed his handsome young face right between her two succulent buttocks, spreading them wide apart with his fingers. Robert began to lick her anus avidly, like a dog. Lola did not utter a word, but instead she backed into his mouth to facilitate the operation, opening her sphincter to admit his tongue as deeply as possible.

Linda felt abandoned. Something which she never liked

---

before. She crept under Robert's legs and began to lap at the tip of his pulsating cock. Her lithe, moist tongue soon forced the erection to its highest pitch.

"Go to it cousin!" The young man's body contorted in pleasure. "Take it in your mouth."

Linda carried out the command and practically swallowed the hardened pole of flesh, sucking on it as hard as she could with her lips tightly round its root. Her tongue slipped over the entire length of his shaft, while his glans leaked strings of pre-come into her throat. The youngster caressed and squeezed his balls, and instinctively scratched his back with her wonderfully painted fingernails. The hand roamed slowly down his backbone and her forefinger, moist with saliva, slipped into his asshole.

She heard the wails of her two partners and from the corner of her eye she saw that Robert was not only licking out Lola's asshole, but her cunt lips as well.

Linda suddenly had an novel idea.

By stretching out on her back she could reach Lola and gain access to her delicious mouth. The tanned woman caught on immediately to the wishes of her younger companion. She complied at once, the pair sucking each other's tongues in deep, sensual kisses, and soon the happy groans of the threesome amplified in the warm air.

In a few minutes they were writhing, tonguing and fingering in rhythm, and their moans formed one large sound that seemed to emanate from one entity.

"Wait a second." Robert interrupted the session, turning toward Linda.

He withdrew his cock from the Linda's slippery mouth and directed the heavy tool toward the rear of squirming Lola, who seemed unhappy at the abrupt change.

"Just watch and learn, kiddo," Robert leered at Linda.

The bright schoolgirl watched with profound curiosity. She was looking at the scene in a topsyturvy position, which added to the sensual aspects and gave the picture an entirely new slant.

Lola backed onto Robert's prick of Robert like a hot filly, and she wiggled wantonly as she attempted to impale her pussy. However, Lola didn't forget Linda for a second, and her tongue was as active as ever. It felt like a soft silk sponge as it gobbled up the youngster's scented cunt juice.

"Now I'm going to fuck the great Lola in the ass. Just watch me, Linda honey."

"Yes... I see... Go ahead, buttfuck her. I want to look on. Robert, give her a good fucking." Linda was happy at her close-up view.

She had no idea what she was saying, she was so excited by her role. She even felt that she was the protagonist of this erotic operation.

Robert aimed his cock right at Lola's asshole and spread her cheeks apart with his big hands in his impatience to begin the lewd act.

Linda didn't lose sight of Robert's actions, and she was almost as excited as he was. She even got in a few last tongue strokes on her cousin's cock, then she helped Lola enjoy herself to the fullest by deeply licking her pussy with her hot mouth.

In this unique position she was able to watch the masterful workings of Robert's cock as it penetrated slowly into the magnificent brunette's rectum.

Robert was half-way inside when Lola began to let out a muffled cry of joy. Linda's mouth was full of sweet juice, cunt juice emitted by the gorgeous woman, who was loosing the floods of her passion by the gallon.

Still working with her tongue, Linda was able to watch Robert's balls knocking up against Lola's buttocks. She gasped as she saw that Robert had buttfucked Lola all the way in to the hilt.

"How nice that looks," she murmured ecstatically.

Lola was grinding her behind against Robert's belly and uttering unintelligible phrases.

Robert was incensed by the muttering and babbling of the lovely brunette. He plunged in and out of her tightly stretched anus like a madman. Linda was inspired by the furious attack, and her avid oral stimulation of Lola's clit drove the older woman into seventh heaven.

"Faster, faster, my pet! Go to it Robert. I want to feel it all the way inside me." Her head bobbed up and down as though she were riding a wild pony.

Robert responded with two or three vigorous strokes.

"She's a real bitch. She's never satisfied. Good old Lola

never gets enough of it. We ought to get a donkey for her..."

Linda heard the infamous words and tried to imagine Lola getting screwed by a mule. She even seemed to see the enormous pizzle of the animal and she couldn't help thinking that such a wicked instrument would certainly give true satisfaction. Linda made a mental note to ask her friend whether diversions of a such nature were prohibited by uncle Arthur. Since he was a demon of the senses, why not indulge in that harmless erotic pastime?

Linda's head spun with curious and fantastic obsessions. She felt that she would never back out of even the most perverse type of erotic pleasure. Perhaps the seeds of the princess that Arthur mentioned were taking fruit.

Just thinking gave her the sudden urge to be penetrated by a fat cock. She wanted something hot, wet and stiff between her legs, and she wanted it quickly.

Desire heightened her perception. She attempted to draw Robert away from Lola. Lola would certainly forgive this ruse by her friend, and anyway she would be able to compensate her in another manner.

Linda disengaged herself from the couple and spread herself out on the bed alongside Lola. Flat on her back with her legs slightly apart, the girl played with the soft hairs of her sex, looking at Robert bewitchingly.

Robert suddenly stopped his movements and he was like a wolf who happened to spot a luscious chunk of raw meat.

"You little whore of a cousin. You want it too, eh?"

"Yes," Linda responded coyly and simply.

"I haven't two cocks, you know? I can't take on two at a time, that's simple isn't it?" Robert said teasingly.

Linda turned toward Lola and took her face and violently kissed her open mouth. Lola reacted to the flame of passion that was a mixture of tenderness, forceful love, and a game.

"Oh, Lola dear. Let me have him for a minute. I want it so badly. Honestly, I need it. It's itching so much. Lola, I do love you terribly – let me have it?"

Lola gave back a passionate tonguing and then looked at the young waif with irony and a storm of passion.

She signalled to Robert.

"Alright Robert, take the little tart. Can't you see she's dying for it?"

Robert laughed. He buffed and bellowed and briskly shoved his cock back into the bronzed beauty's asshole.

"What do you think I am, your servant? Do you think I have to obey you without having the right to choose for myself?"

Lola wasn't fooled by the play Robert put on. She saw that he was attracted by her cousin as she spread-eagled herself on the bed, panting away with lust. The boy just wanted to tease the girl and make her long for him all the more.

Linda was taken in by the game. In fact, she grabbed the boy's arm and pleaded with him hysterically.

"Please Robert, please... I want to be... I *crave* to be fucked by you..."

Robert pulled out his prick from the two cheeks of Lola's rump. Linda watched it as though she were spellbound by its movements. Hypnotized by this rigid snake streaked with shit and dribbling thick milky strands of come, she thought she would go mad with the need to have it inside her.

Suddenly she seized it with her hand and forced Robert to take the necessary step. Lola, who was on her side, pushed the boy by his buttocks toward the beckoning girl. Robert didn't wait any longer, and in a trice he managed to impale his cousin with his abnormally swollen cock. Lola her eyes inflamed, was delighted to watch the two writhe in heated pleasure.

Robert pumped away with force and unbridled passion, till at last he felt his balls exploding and he whipped his cock out of Linda's cunt, spraying great gouts of hot spunk onto his cousin's startled face.

chapter seven

A half-an-hour later, the three were stretched out on the bed. Robert was in between his two mistresses. Lola's and Linda's hands met while they tickled and stroked the balls and penis of the happy young man, who was peacefully reclined with his hands in back of his head. He let the girls do what they wished, while he closed his eyes and beamed contentment all over his boyish face.

"I really must say that this young scamp has a certain talent for his gangly age. Don't you think I'm right, Linda dear?"

Linda merely smiled and continued to caress her cousin's ball sac.

"Tell me Robert, when did you first make love? When was the very first time you properly possessed a woman?" Lola asked the boy questions because she was truly inquisitive. She had an admiration for the younger generation and their precocity, and wanted to know their ways.

"I guess I was fourteen. That's right, I remember. I wasn't more than fourteen. I did it with Edith, my sister. Do you know her Linda?"

"Yes. I saw her once at aunt Martha's in London about three years ago."

"Tell us what happened," Lola coaxed the lad.

"Well, we were by the sea near Atlantic City – Edith, Rita, my youngest sister and my mother. Edith at the time was nineteen and Rita was fourteen, or nearly fourteen. Edith was, and still is for that matter, very attractive with her brown tresses and her tigerish body. Her ass is perfectly formed and her teats are just as they should be. When she walks down the street she has everyone's head turning, men and women alike.

"One day I decided to take a long walk along the waterfront. I think I wanted to be alone, because I walked a good deal.

I headed for the little cabin we had near the north shore. For miles around you couldn't hear a living soul. Nearing the cabin I heard some noise.

"Being by nature quite curious, I decided to sneak up and see what it was all about. Through a small crack in the wood I was able to spy Edith, my svelte sister, stretched out on the floor completely nude. There was a man on top of her and I recognized him to be the young architect that had been flirting with her since we had come to the beach. He was looming over her in a lewd position, and Edith seemed to be enjoying the taste of his 'thing'. I watched for a few seconds and then drew away as softly as I had come. I hid in the nearby bushes.

"Ten minutes later the architect had left the cabin, apparently afraid of being caught by our mother. But I knew no-one was going to come before noon, and it was hardly ten o'clock."

"And what did you do then?" Linda asked, following his story with interest and awaiting a denouement to the intriguing tale.

"Once he had left, I went back to the cabin. I opened the door and I saw Edith still lying on the floor, obviously tired from her violent efforts. When she regained her senses and saw me, she tried to hide her nudity. She asked with surprise what I was doing there at such an early hour.

"'You made love quite well, sis,' I said, tossing it off as if it were the most natural thing to say. She looked at me with hate in her eyes. 'Get the hell out of here. I want to dress.' This was her vulgar response. I tried my luck and said, 'You don't have to get dressed for what you're going to do. If not, I'm going to tell mother the truth – and she is not going to like that, is she?' She was thunderstruck. 'You're out of your head.' Then with a little more conviction she called me a dirty little pig and pushed me away.

"I held my stand and told her she was nothing but a slut herself, and that if she would make love with me, I wouldn't breathe a word."

Edith didn't say a word. She just stared at me resignedly. I undressed nervously, and then threw myself on her like a young lion. 'Take it easy, little brother. This is where you have to get in.' She took my prick with her hand and felt its hardness. Adeptly she slipped it into her wet vagina. Then she shifted around and made it all the harder. Her movements were so well-accomplished that inside a few seconds I came with all my might. My first thought was that it was much, much better than masturbating at the cinema. Several of my friends would hold a masturbating session when we watched a sexy film. You know, we would change around and masturbate each other, or suck each other off in the dark.

"It seemed that Edith had a penchant toward incest, because to my surprise that same evening she asked me to come up to her room and recommence the same business we had taken up that morning. She taught me the sweet pleasure of sucking and being sucked. We spent the whole night making love."

"And then what happened?" Lola wanted to know everything as she stroked Robert's massive cock.

"Afterwards, everything came naturally. I can even remember the first experience of this type that I had with Rita. One evening she was sleeping and I tip-toed into her room like a thief. She had pushed her covers aside and she was sleeping naked because it was a hot summer's night. I woke her by placing my hand on her pussy. She has that silken type of hair that curls gently, a bit like yours Linda. Naturally she cried out in alarm, but was less frightened to see her brother. She said she had been dreaming and thought it might be a burglar. I reassured her and told her not to be afraid. I told her a fib about losing my key and that I would have to sleep with her that night. I pretended to be annoyed at my misfortune. At first she didn't like the idea, but seeing that her brother was hard put (in fact, I was growing hard by the minute), she relented. Until then, we had the normal relationship between brother and sister and she wasn't in the least suspicious about anything out of the norm. She rolled over and covered herself, while I lay down by her side."

"My, you're slow getting to the point," said Linda, pressing and squeezing the head of her cousin's cock.

"A few minutes later, I began to caress her softly. She moved away and told me not too be so intimate with her. She was sure I was just teasing her and she played the part of someone annoyed. She told me she wanted to sleep and to keep my roving hands to myself. Suddenly I jumped on top of her and pushed her legs apart. My cock was ready and with a bit of effort I managed to penetrate her. In spite of her young age she wasn't a virgin. When she understood that I was serious in my endeavour, she submitted willingly. The little darling of a sister loved to be fucked, and the following nights she didn't fail to come to my room to get screwed in the many fashions that Edith had taught me. Even now when we see each other, we never hesitate in taking advantage of our feverish desires.

Rita told me that she lost her virginity at thirteen. She was alone in the house one day when a man knocked on the door. He was a lowly butcher and she was ready to close the door on him after taking his package, when the man jumped her and forced her to the couch in the living room. Rita told me that in spite of the pain she found the whole act extremely satisfactory. She adored the manner in which he had violated her. I had always thought that Rita was a little devil, and this story confirmed my opinion.

"She told me that no-one but me knows about it. Since that time, and before I tried it with her, she had been screwed twice by strangers in brief encounters. All the boys of her own age irritated her, and she found no joy in being with them."

Linda couldn't help thinking of how Robert and his sisters were advanced for their ages, and how they made good use of their very young lives to taste the pleasures of fucking and sucking.

"So that's the way it is? You made love with your sisters in such a disgusting, incestuous way. What a family, what shame," Lola laughed, teasing the young man.

"And why not? If you had a brother with a prick that you liked, would you say no?". Robert got back at Lola with this slight chiding.

"I haven't got a brother, so I don't know how to respond." Lola tickled his balls.

"I think we ought to hurry up, if we want to take a bath before lunch." Linda took the initiative. An improvised after midnight feast was called 'lunch' in this strange household where every hour was a vibrant period of pleasure.

"You're right, Linda. We had better hurry," Lola chimed in.

"Wait a minute. You're not going to leave me in this state after playing around with my nuts for a half-hour."

Robert showed the two young ladies his powerful phallus, which had sprung up like a flag-pole while he was telling the filthy story of his sisters' antics. He waggled the tool under the eyes of Lola and Linda.

"We're in a rush. We don't have time to busy ourselves with your cause." Lola laughed uproariously on seeing Robert's cock twitch with frustration.

"Hey, I know what you can do. Both of you can suck on it at once, and that way it will be over quicker."

The two friends agreed with feigned reluctance, just to tease the lad, and then bent their heads toward his erection. Lola was the first to take in a mouthful, and Linda had to be content with the lad's balls, which were quite swollen with lust. Then they changed round and Linda eased her mouth over the hot cock while Lola nibbled at the sac beneath.

Robert let out a groan of delight and his two hands sunk into the girls' hair and he patted them on their excellent work.

He was obsessed with the marvellous idea of the two girls who were applying their art for his sole benefit. In his mind's eye he saw his two sisters working him over, and this intensified his pleasure as though he were being ravished by *four* lovely women of different ages.

"Quicker, my dears, faster... I'm co... I'm goingggg to come!" He shrieked out his ecstasy.

It was Linda who still had the fat prick in her mouth and she sucked on it with both force and affection. She ran her tongue along the shaft then flicked around the glans. Her cousin's stories had put her in a frenzy that she had never known before. The scene reached a raging climax, Robert moaning feverishly as he threw his head backwards and he ejaculated. She felt the hot spunk jet into her mouth, flooding her throat.

Lola wanted to get some of the juice, and she took Linda's place in the dying moments of Robert's pleasure, sucking up the very last drops. The two bitches had taken an equal share of liquid and they both swallowed it at the same time, as Robert's eyes popped with floating, unutterable delight.

Then, to show how much they appreciated the young lad, they cleaned him out entirely with their long tongues, Linda washing out his anus with deep circular licking while Lola saw to the inside of his inflamed foreskin before grooming his pubic hair.

chapter eight

Early in the morning Linda finally went to bed, tired but satisfied. She spent the next morning at the beach with Lola and Robert, and then later on with uncle Arthur and Alice at the villa. They all ate together and then everyone went his or her separate way, except Linda wound up with Lola and Robert.

The day was spent in resting up. Lola drove Linda to the strand, a thin layer of beach, which offered a splendid view. Linda was able to admire the setting sun under the soft caresses of the tiger lady, Lola. When the two friends came back to the house, they were laughing jovially and appeared to be in an exceptional frame of mind.

"Good night, Lola." Linda gave the sentence an added twist in the hope of having Lola with her that night.

"Nighty-night," Lola responded, with an odd exuberant smile. She even added a mean phrase that was not at all warranted, but it was just Lola's way of taunting the girl.

"Have fun, dear."

Linda felt sure that Lola was just being ironic, thinking that the young girl was going to masturbate before catching her beauty sleep. But little did Lola guess that the precocious schoolgirl wanted something else than the simple process of jerking off in her bed.

However, Linda was not discontent to find her room warm and snug. She undressed herself and walked over to the window for some fresh air and to admire the full moon that sprayed its light over the bed.

Then she heard the noise of several automobiles arriving at the villa, and she wondered who on earth could be calling at such an hour, when everyone was almost asleep.

With the curiosity of a cat she went to the door and heard her uncle greet the new arrivals.

Gosh, he's awake, Linda said to herself, almost out loud.

She opened the door a little to hear the conversation between her uncle and his friends.

"You're late," Arthur reproached the newcomers.

"We had trouble with the car." It was a woman who spoke.

The others, men and women, laughed at the seemingly inoffensive words. Linda put on a night dress and silently went to the foot of the stairs. She wanted to see what they looked like.

Luckily she was able to glance down into the living room, where she saw four men, one the age of her uncle and the others a bit younger. She also counted three women, two who were approximately twenty-five and a third who was no more than sixteen. The youngest was the one with the heartiest laughter. She had a vibrant, attractive body which was highlighted by the pullover clinging to her upper body and a yellow skirt that accentuated the curves of her torso.

Linda noticed that they all spoke informally, and she was sure that they were good friends of her uncle. Compelled to see better, Linda courageously descended a few steps. She watched her uncle, who was pouring liquor in their glasses. Then he sat next to the gamine in the yellow skirt and put his arm around her waist, which looked slim and firm.

"And you, Annie? In good form tonight?"

"Tip-top. And you, grandpa?" She was brazen and Linda didn't see how the girl dared to respond in this manner. Linda was then astonished to see the young girl put her hand between Arthur's legs. Arthur merely laughed and placed his mouth right on the nipple of the girl's left breast and bit into it sharply.

"Ouch! Edgar, your friend is a brute."

The man named Edgar drank his whiskey calmly and then put down his glass.

"Where's Lola, Arthur? Isn't she going to come down?"

"In a little while. Don't be impatient. By the way, we have another guest. My niece."

Linda instinctively perked up her ears and listened intently.

"What's she like?" one of the men asked.

"You'll see her presently," Arthur said, unaware that his curious niece was quite present already.

They all began to drink one glass of whiskey after another.

One of the two older women, a brunette who was rather tall and well-stacked, was reclining. Right by her was one of the four men, who caressed her legs pulling her skirt high up on her milky thighs. The other woman, blonde-haired and nervous, was seated in a large armchair between two men. The fourth man, named Edgar, remained alone in a leather armchair by the window.

At that moment Alice arrived with a tray of sandwiches. She came in barefooted with a short apron that barely reached her knees, and one could guess that she had little or nothing on underneath.

She put the tray on the table and came up to Edgar, who grabbed her by the waist and made her sit on his lap.

"Come, my little one. I want to make an exploration. Don't worry, it will be very personal and precise."

And he began to put his hands under Alice's apron. Alice pretended to run away and she broke out in a peel of laughter. But the man discovered her nude thighs and then unveiled her breasts, which jumped out as though they were expecting that treatment all along.

"Just look at these marvels, everybody." He held the maid up for all to see.

He leaned down and sucked on one and then the other tit, just to capture their warmth and flavour.

"I defy any of you women to show a better pair. Is there anyone who wants to complete?"

Annie perked up anxiously. She sprang to her feet and immediately exclaimed: "Well how about these, for example?"

She brusquely pealed off her pullover, and two splendid young teats popped out in all their gravity-defying majesty. They were firm as two coconut halves. The men applauded.

"Bravo!" Arthur shouted.

And he took Annie by force and brought her close to his sinewy body. He placed his mouth on the nipple of one rosebud tit and tongued the sweet teenage flesh.

"And what about you others? Helen, Christine? We're waiting, and it isn't fair to keep us waiting, you know." Edgar was eager to see some action.

Helen, the large brunette, responded with a chuckle. The fellow who was sitting at her side put his hand underneath her blouse, while the other was already busy masturbating the pink-faced lady. She abandoned herself with half-closed eyes. The blonde, Christine, took up the challenge. She stripped down with an indifferent air and turned to everyone with a blasé expression.

"Don't you think we are all prudes? We are definitely wearing too much. Let's not be so ridiculous."

She let her dress fall to the ground. She didn't have a stitch of underclothing on. Linda, from her advantageous hiding place, thought – and justly so – that the women had prepared for the evening. It was bound to wind up in a real spectacle. Linda was feverish with excitement.

"It's our turn men. The evening has begun rather quickly tonight, so let's make the best of it."

"Alright fellows," another added. "Edgar, Nick, Stephen and Arthur – everything off."

And they all answered the call. The women were anxious to see the cocks of the four gentlemen, who were just as immodest as the females present.

Linda had her eyes bulging out as she watched the men undress themselves hastily. When they were all nude, she saw that the friends of her uncle all had a prick of gigantic proportions. She especially noticed Edgar's. His powerful brown weapon was menacing Alice. Linda tried to imagine the feel of such an enormous cock in her vagina. And she almost cried aloud when she thought of the same tool attempting to enter her anus.

The festival, or orgy, or whatever one wished to call it, was decidedly on the way. Linda observed the antics of the revellers. Edgar already had Alice on the carpet, having ripped off her flimsy apron. The little maid squirmed lasciviously on the plush covering like a mink in all splendour.

The petite servant girl showed her long svelte thighs in all their glory. Her two teats stood up and greeted her handsome violater and her smooth belly undulated like the ripple of splashing water. Her bush of curly pubic hair seemed electrified Edgar bore down upon her. The man's face fell upon her pungent pussy like a hungry fox, and he plunged his inflamed tongue deep within her lips of pleasure.

Annie didn't hesitate to duplicate matters, and even improve upon them. She knelt before Arthur and took his sturdy prick straight in her small oval mouth. The youngster emitted lewd noises as she slobbered away with the engorged cock plugged deep in her mouth.

The teenager had not as yet taken off her tight skirt, and it was Nick who took the initiative on unzipping the garment and pushing it to the floor. It was evident that he wished to have part of the girl for himself. Annie did not increase nor decrease her sucking. She just was concerned with her job and apparently she enjoyed it, from the look on Arthur's face.

The man who was called Stephen was still occupied with Helen, who was laid out on the divan with open thighs. The girl had a body that was meant to be sculpted. She resembled a statue with her fine muscular torso.

Stephen had the large woman on her belly and she arched up, enabling him to lick her asshole. Linda covered her mouth to keep from giggling when she saw how the young lady was grimacing at her awkward position.

Nick mounted Christine as soon as she was available. His cock was fat and rigid and the blonde girl was moaning with pleasure in no time.

Linda was watching the extraordinary coupling of partners when she heard footsteps behind her. Turning around, she saw Lola who stopped a few feet away from her. Undoubtedly she had been looking in on Arthur's guests too, for there was a sardonic smile on her lips.

Lola had put on her yellow pyjamas and she put her finger to her lips in a signal of silence. Then she tip-toed over to Linda.

"It's entertaining, isn't it? Have you been here for a long time?"

"Since they arrived. Why have they come here?" Linda asked.

Lola laughed silently. She whispered in Linda's pretty ear.

"It's just a little party that your uncle has organized. But what we are seeing is only the aperitif."

"The aperitif?"

"I mean it is only the beginning. They're just warming up, rubbing against one another and lightly making love. But the best is yet to come. Naturally you're invited."

"Me?" Linda was surprised to hear this.

She glanced at the people in the salon and her eyes immediately fell on Edgar's prick. The young man was busy tickling Alice's ear. Linda was surprised at the sudden feeling that gripped her. She was envious of Alice and she would have changed places with her at the drop of a hat. Lucky Alice had that wonderful, juicy cock at her beck and call.

Lola was delighted to see that Linda took such pleasure in the party. The older woman was able to read the young girl's thoughts, and she made a proposition.

"Yes, of course, you can participate in the party, because you are the attraction that Arthur promised his guests. In one way, that's why they're here. You will be screwed and buttfucked by all the men. They will do what they wish with you, and you'll be happy to give in. Doesn't that give you goose pimples, just to think of all the hot cocks you'll feel in you?"

Linda trembled on hearing these words, but her eyes remained glued to the scene below. She secretly anticipated the delicious treats that were in store for her.

"I didn't tell you about the women. What a bunch of hot bitches in heat *they* are. They wouldn't hesitate to put their hands in their fathers' pants. They'll throw themselves on you like a pack of wolves. One month ago Annie, the youngest, brought her thirteen-year-old sister to one of these shindigs. She did it on purpose, in order to pervert her sister who she always loved and hated at the same time. The poor kid, although she was good-looking, was raped by your uncle and buttfucked by Edgar. Then they all got in their licks. The girl must have been sodomized at least twelve or thirteen times. The morning after she could hardly walk and her asshole was bleeding. She had to stay here, after giving a weak excuse to her parents. But I suspect her of being a regular nymphomaniac, just like her sister. She doesn't let a day go by without flirting with any man she picks up. Once in a while she stalks them down in the street like a whore."

Lola spoke luridly, and her words excited Linda who was visibly moved by what the brunette had to say. Her eyes were filled with bright fascination.

In the living room, the scene had changed slightly. Arthur had put Annie on his knees and he was just starting to stick his cock into the girl's tiny asshole. At once, Linda saw the big dick disappear, in one gulp, into the red anus. Annie jumped in the air as though she had been stung by a bee. And Edgar was doing the same to Alice, but in a different fashion. He had the maid lie on the floor, point her feet to the ceiling and hang on to her ankles. Edgar dug underneath and met her anus with his beautiful prick. It seemed to Linda that Alice, who was normally used to such an operation, was not taking the huge cock as well as she usually did. Suddenly Linda realized that while she was watching Edgar and Alice go through the act of sodomy, she was idly masturbating herself. Nevertheless she continued, in spite of Lola's amused look.

Stephen made Christine submit by employing a treatment that usually has a good deal of success with young girls. He had her lying on her side and he slipped his slender cock into her vagina from behind. He had slyly unhooked a candle, and Linda saw that it was wiggling in Christine's asshole. The lucky girl was being serviced by two rigid instruments. Although she let out a piercing cry, it was apparent that she was enjoying herself by the smile on her face. She was even on the verge of coming, judging by the way her pussy was discharging its juice. Then Christine emitted a long groan, her pelvis and buttocks bucking, and she managed to be the first to come. Teenager Annie was next in line.

Linda noticed that she was extremely wet between the thighs. She had come herself, but she had so fixed her attention on the others that she had not noticed her own arousal. In fact, she was astonished at seeing the clear white liquid drip to the floor.

"Well, that isn't nice, is it? I think it's time for us to take part in the game, don't you?" Lola took Linda firmly by the arm and led her downstairs. The young girl was flushed. Lola went down the steps so rapidly that Linda almost lost her breath.

"Hey everyone! Here she is. The guest of honour."

Everybody looked at her, appraising her from head to foot.

Edgar was the first to break the silence, while he held on firmly to Alice who was snugly lodged underneath him. He said he approved of the guest, and beamed with delight.

"Well if it isn't our Lola, Lolalita. And the other must be the famous niece we've heard so much about. And, I might add, not without good reason!"

"Come along, princess. Don't be timid. Nobody here will bite you... yet." Uncle Arthur proudly took the girl's hand.

Linda pulled down her nightie, which just barely reached her knees. Lola pushed her toward the group and soon Linda found herself surrounded by the many guests.

"Well, what's the verdict, ladies and gentlemen? Shall we adopt her or not?"

"She looks like the kind who would go for our antics," Nick said with a scrupulous air.

He continued to masturbate Helen while the blonde sucked him off, ogling the newcomer. Normally she would be busy with Arthur's cock, which she loved.

Lola and Linda had arrived at the right time and they gave a certain enthusiasm to the group, who livened up and began to show their gratitude.

Nick unplugged his cock long enough to demonstrate its proportions to Linda, who could not take her eyes off it. It was covered with saliva and had attained a length that was quite impressive. He brandished it like a conquering hero.

"Let's see what she can do," Stephen hollered out.

Nick unbuttoned Linda's pale nightie. Soon she was nude and her nipples grew hard at once. Her little bush of hair glittered in the candlelight of the living room. The young girl looked at Lola helplessly.

Lola was already seated between Arthur and Helen. They sat like three majesties on the divan, deciding the fate of the modest schoolgirl.

"She's kind of young." Nick offered his opinion as he brought the girl close to his nude, hairy body. "But I think she has promise. As for me, I'm ready to take her apart right now. Are there any objections?"

"Go ahead, my boy. But remember, I'm the one that is going to take her from behind," Edgar boasted, thumping his chest like a hunter.

Alice was somewhat jealous, and she dragged her buttfucker back to the position he had neglected while contemplating future delights.

Annie, the little nympho, approached Linda and fixed her on the spot with a cruel smile.

"I have a proposition to make all of you. While you two take her from the front and the back, she is going to lick me out."

Linda listened to all of this without even trying to get a word in edgewise. She was intimidated by the numbers, and she was too emotionally disturbed to offer any resistance.

"Let's have a little order in our meeting, ladies and gentlemen, if I may call you that." Arthur proved that he was the organizer and chairman of the whole affair. In his usual, amiable way he dominated the situation with his fatherly smile.

"Now, my niece is all yours, just as I had promised. And you can do as you like with her. But I am going to offer you a proposition. First of all, the men are going to treat her with their cocks. She'll be had from the front by Nick, and Edgar can have her the way he suggested. Stephen and myself will receive her best kisses. Don't worry about her youngish air. She can take all you fellows have to offer." He bade them on, and wished them all good luck.

Linda, still in the clutches of Nick who was feeling her up more and more, had her anus plugged by one of his fingers. She realised that it would be impossible to escape her fate. She had to face up to it. Her mission was to satisfy all the men and, probably, all the women in the group.

"And what about us?" Helen spoke out. Linda prepared for the worst.

Lola stripped down and she was lying on the couch next to Arthur like the queen of Sheba. A cigarette hung from her full lips.

"Don't be in such a rush, dear," Arthur laughed amusedly.

"I'll take care of her," Annie said with lust flaming in her eyes.

"Oh, no, Annie, we'll take care of you ourselves. You had your night a few weeks back. You must learn to give way to others. Egoism is a terrible sin, you know."

Arthur managed to keep the hungry women in cheek, but he was wondering just how long he could hold out with such a pack of she-wolves. He laughed heartily and it was quite clear that he was the master of his own household. He had to be diplomatic about it all, and he decided to use tact.

"Let's all be calm. I'm going to find someone who will be able to help us out."

Arthur had already spotted Robert coming down the stairs. The lad was nude and he had the same ironic and luxurious smile as usual. He saluted everyone, being familiar with the clan for many months now.

"I see that my cousin is up for the slaughter. Well, that's the way the big ball bounces. Good luck Linda, honey."

"Robert, sugar." Annie snuggled up to the young fellow and cooed in his ear with her best capricious, baby-doll voice. "You'll take care of me, won't you? Your uncle seems to forget all about me."

"Why you little liar! Just a minute ago I had my penis in your asshole, and you've got the nerve to complain. Well, that's a woman for you..."

"Let's stop beating around the bush. Do whatever you want all of you – but I'm going to start off with a healthy chunk. That delicious, pink asshole is all mine, gentlemen." Edgar was the first to start the ball rolling.

He disengaged his cock from Alice's rump. It was slick and steaming. The young maid received such a shock at this withdrawal that she remained non-plussed and gaping on the floor, waiting for someone to replace her lover.

Edgar approached Linda, who almost crossed her eyes gazing at his enormous, threatening prick. This was the man who had excited her imagination. With the gigantic proportions and the purple head sticking high above two testicles as large as tennis balls, the cock was ringed in brown matter all along the shaft. It was the shit of little Alice.

"He'll kill me with that thing if he puts it in my rear," thought Linda, who was turning green with worry.

Nick folded her legs back and made her sit on the floor.

"Wait a minute Eddie. She should be comfortable to get the best out of it." Nick carefully put the girl in the prescribed position.

Then he took a pillow from the divan and placed it under the girl's sweet buttocks.

"Isn't that better now, my angel?"

Edgar tipped his huge cock along the rim of the girl's mouth and then stroked her on both cheeks with the heavy glans. Linda inhaled the pungent odour of the soiled phallus. The horrible scent gave the girl an added thrill, and she slowly prepared herself for the double violation.

Exquisitely, her tongue nipped out and darted at the rigid

cock. She closed her eyes and a smile brightened on her youthful face.

Stephen and Arthur came over, and Linda was soon encircled by four great pricks, purplish flesh throbbing in unison.

Christine and Annie came over to join in the fun. They watched the luxurious setting unfold and their lovely eyes rolled with excited curiosity.

"Everyone ready?" Nick set the starting signal.

"Just a second, Edgar. I'd like to lubricate her hole so that it will be all prepared for the feast."

Stephen bent down and licked the teenager's asshole. She rolled over in a wave of sensual agitation, pushing her anus back over his tongue. Christine turned red with envy.

"Get away from her. I'll do it."

"As you wish, *mademoiselle*, but do hurry."

"Say, what about me?" Helen's voice boomed out from the dark corner in the back of the room.

She came running over to the spot where the lascivious procedures were taking place. Helen and Christine gave curvaceous Linda the once over, and they didn't miss a point on her splendid body. The two women stuck to her like leeches. Christine rotated her tongue in the tight pink hole of her backside, while Helen expertly, slowly licked out her pussy. Every once in a while she would look up wide-eyed at the others, to let them know that she was enjoying herself. The others were vexed, envious and obviously becoming frustrated.

Christine began to cough because she had stuck her tongue so far up Linda's asshole. The anal vent was flooded with warm saliva and its sweet odour permeated the room. Helen was meticulously working on the front with the half-happy and half-indifferent air she usually presented. She made sucking noises as she rigorously tongue-fucked the swooning schoolgirl.

Linda flexed her muscles in pleasure and her head bobbed up and down like a cork floating on blue waters. The whites of her eyes showed to such an extent that all were wondering when her blue eyes would ever come back into her lovely head.

The men were growing impatient, and when their cries went unheeded they were forced to drag the girls away. But the females refused to give up their terrain and they fought the men tooth and nail. Arthur and Robert were obliged to haul them away by the roots of their hair. They took them into the parlour and satisfied them with various combinations of sodomy and cunt-sucking.

Alice and Annie joined them, while imperious Lola sat comfortably in an armchair, her arms folded and not the slightest expression in her beautiful bronze face.

The four men had managed to place Linda in the desired position, and Nick once more led the festivities. He swung one of her free legs in the air and lowered his head to the slippery, wide-open cunt. Nick decided that he would be more at home there with his cock, so he placed his hard-on at the opening. He groaned with satisfaction as the glans settled against her hot pussy lips, and then moaned his contentment when he slid deep inside the rose-coloured crevice.

"Are you ready at your end, Edgar?"

Nick was a good fellow, always thinking of others.

"Go on lad. Let's get down to work. You know the saying, talk is cheap."

Edgar slipped behind the delirious girl, who was prone on the floor but still managed an acrobatic half-turn to present her plump little buttocks, a sight which stiffened Edgar's cock by a good two inches.

Nick held her on her side while Edgar dipped down and fingered the anus. His large hands cupped the two halves of her gorgeous rump, pulling them apart, and he aimed his heavy penis at the shining asshole as it spread slowly open.

Linda jiggled for a second and then remained perfectly still, anticipating the penetration of her next lover. Then all of a sudden, she felt a human crow-bar burst into her tiny hole. Instead of riding the blow, she backed into it all the more and took the invading cock in full stride, sucking it deep inside her entrails to the very hilt.

Linda almost fainted on the spot. Edgar crashed into her asshole with his massive cock and Nick held fast, never giving more than a half centimetre of ground. The fainting schoolgirl was speared fore and aft, and the two men's cocks rubbed together on each side of her vaginal membrane.

A trickle of blood flowed down the thigh of the limp girl, and it was apparent that her asshole had widened by a good inch.

She was half-unconscious in her struggle between pain and pleasure.

Edgar got all the more excited at the red streaks. He loved the tightness of her back-passage, but at the moment the young lady wasn't giving back any bumps and grinds. To liven her up a bit, he dug his shaft in to the hilt. Linda screeched in pain and then threw her cunt over to Nick, who ploughed into it with renewed gusto.

The two men felt each other pumping as they plunged deep within the confines of the schoolgirl's asshole and pussy. Due to the tightness and the compact structure of the girl's lower body, the two men were practically masturbating each other within the hot, wet hollows of her pelvis. Poor Linda felt blasted by the massive pricks, which were gaining momentum by the minute. She had a vague thought of how and where was it all going to end, but slowly she lost consciousness and the muscles of her thighs went dead as she sank into an unprecedented faint.

"What good is she? She can't take on two for a damn. Quick Arthur, get some smelling salts for your niece. The girl is croaking, old chap."

Arthur was too busy filling Helen's mouth with his prick to be bothered by such trivial incidents. The oblivious uncle hollered back his disgruntled feelings.

"Whack her a few times. She'll come around in no time."

Lola saw the distress of the two husky men and decided to take matters in her own hands.

From a drawer in Arthur's desk she brought out a thin flexible whip. She tapped Edgar on the shoulder with it, and he quickly got the hint. Both men leaned away, though they remained firmly buried inside the dazed girl. Lola unhooked some terrifying blows that brought Linda back to life in no time flat. The girl thought she would go out of her mind from the sting of the brutalizing whip. After a dozen well-aimed strokes, she gathered all her strength and tossed her body backward and forward trying to ward off the gnawing anguish of the lash.

But she was pinned by the two lovers who were tightly bound within. Suddenly, as the sting of Lola's blows connected with the raw nerves of her engorged orifices, she received a shock of pleasure which ran up her spinal cord.

Linda bucked and spun along the tickling carpet, as she

started to grind away with her two lovers. For the first time, she gave way to the growing enjoyment that burned at her insides. Nick pistoned in and out of her pussy and then Edgar picked up the rhythm with his anal thrusts, and all three fused into a mass of pulsating flesh. Meanwhile Lola kept up her punishment and even wielded her strokes on the luckless men. The didn't seem to mind though, and it even appeared as though the flogging was pushing them on to new heights.

"Now you'll have me, my darling, just like you were supposed to. Come on honey, grind away and do it properly. How are things on your end, Nick old boy?"

"Just fine, Edgar."

Linda relaxed and more than enjoyed herself. Her full lips gasped out moans of delight as she sucked away at Nick's earlobe. She winced with crazed sensual ecstasy as Edgar tongued her back and bit into her shoulder blade.

"Oh darling, gouge me out. You're big, my lover, and I love it. Oh, how I love it. You'll never know."

Her little pussy spasmed in synchronized rhythm as the two men gave all their energy to the luscious flesh which bound them.

It was a rare sight to see the young girl with her innocent asshole stuffed with a full-sized cock, while at the same time her snatch took a battering which threatened to split it apart.

Stephen and Arthur had come back, and they were insisting that the two fellows who were doing such an excellent job should now give up their turns. Nick and Edgar were reluctant to do so.

They were screwing and buttfucking Linda furiously, and besides, they were right in the swing of things. There was no good reason why they should relinquish their rights.

"Shall we pull out, Linda? Others are waiting and they don't seem to like the idea that we are getting all the honey."

"Tell them to go to hell." Linda responded vulgarly but justly so, for right at that moment she felt her pussy swelling with the pangs of a huge impending orgasm.

"Stick with us baby, and we'll fuck you to the stars." Nick was full of filthy talk as he prepared to explode.

Suddenly Linda thought she was going to suffocate. The two men crushed her between them and she felt their muscular bodies stiffen in an effort to retain their colossal climaxes.

"I think I've had it, Edgar! I'mm comminggggg There it is – Ahhhhhhhhh!" Nick unleashed his hot spunk into the far depths of Linda's cunt.

Linda jiggled up and down, and noticed Lola watching the proceedings with those panther-like eyes of hers. She wondered what the woman was thinking of as she felt the warm wave of come invade her lower belly.

In the meantime, Robert had come over and like the spoiled lad who was, stuck his cock straight into Linda's open mouth. She only had it open to breath better. But Linda didn't complain. She felt that it was just an added gift of male flesh, and should be consumed with gratitude. She started sucking on it as if it were a stick of candy, running her tongue up and down the shaft.

Meanwhile she refused to let Nick out of her pussy, and she milked his cock with her cunt muscles, keeping him semi-erect. She felt Edgar still slithering in and out of her soaking asshole.

Her mad tongue rolled around Robert's cock, which had grown to amazing proportions; the youngster was on the verge of a premature orgasm – much to his shame.

All at once, Robert blew out his sperm and it forced Linda's mouth to swell like a balloon. The girl valiantly kept the cock in her mouth as she gulped down the hot liquid.

Robert shook like a young lamb at a slaughter. His head flung back, he bellowed his approval while digging his fingers into Linda's wild silky hair.

Edgar was next. He didn't come all at once, but instead he throbbed out his white jism like a machine gun issues bullets.

Every time he let loose, Linda's rump expanded. The girl was in the throes of her third orgasm, and the deliberately slow manner in which Edgar was holding back gave the delirious girl hope of a fourth.

"You look like a perfect little angel," Lola said, and then howled with laughter. She had to hold her hand over her mouth to keep from startling everyone.

Suddenly Linda began to hiccup. Perhaps it was out of guilt, or perhaps it was due to Lola's mockery. Robert was inclined to believe that she swallowed too much of his sperm. Half of it had already gushed down her throat, while the rest of it was overflowing from her soft lips.

Nick finally disengaged his thoroughly tired prick from her sodden pussy. Robert followed suit when he saw that Edgar was reaching back on the small table to get at a cigarette. His limp cock fell from Linda's asshole, which was distended and overflowing with red- and brown-streaked jism.

Linda, completely fatigued, crawled over to where Lola was sitting.

"How was it, lovie? You seemed to be having a whale of a time."

"You'll never know. Oh, Lola... I lost count. Was it four or five?... It was unbelievable... just like a dream. I'd have never thought that it could be like that."

Lola patted her head and glanced at her peacefully.

"There are no complaints, then. But we've only just started. Much is yet to come!"

Lola took Linda by the hand and led her back to the group. Robert was trying to buttfuck Alice, while Arthur was getting in his best strokes on the spread-eagled Helen. He was pinching her teats while he plunged his big prick into her well-lubricated asshole. They were both on their way to having silent, powerful ejaculations.

"They haven't finished yet. I don't think we should disturb them, do you? Besides, it doesn't look as though they will be detained for long." Lola laughed playfully.

"Let's get started with the second half of the show." Edgar rubbed his hands.

"What second half?" Linda asked, looking somewhat puzzled.

Lola laughed and tapped her on the shoulders. "Don't be impatient. You'll see, and you'll *feel* much better about it."

Lola seemed to be having her private joke.

Linda watched the woman's face in its multiple expressions. She wondered just what surprise Lola had in store for her, and why she was chuckling like a wicked witch.

---

chapter nine

Linda gazed at Lola's bewitching belly. She watched the curly hair wind up from the crotch, and then she caught Lola's glance.

"May I?" Linda asked humbly.

After the terrible assault by the male members of the party, Linda was happy to return to the sanctified domain of womanhood.

Lola spread open her thighs and Linda's head lowered to meet the sweet-scented pussy. The young girl began to lick at the cunt-lips and clit like a puppy.

"You're a love, you know?" Lola whispered to Linda's bobbing head.

All the men present stood around and watched the two lascivious ladies. They were tired and rightfully felt that Lola's patience merited some consideration. Then they sank in the chairs and on the sofas, each one showing signs of his recent fatigue.

Annie was the first to perk up and make suggestion.

"Let's dance. I feel like moving around a little. Come on, don't be a bunch of stiffs."

"Come here and move around on this." Stephen tapped his cock and roared with a hoarse laughter.

"A little later darling. First of all, I want some music. Something that will give the place atmosphere and mood."

She went over to the phonograph and chose a waltz. This gave Edgar the opportunity to dance with Linda. He graciously took the young girl in his husky arms and they stepped elegantly to the bursting pleasure of music.

Linda felt his prick hard and ready for action. She clung to him like a ship-wrecked victim. Soon they were not the only ones who were dancing. Arthur held Annie in his arms, while Stephen tripped the light fantastic with Lola. Nick picked up Helen and Robert had his hands wrapped around Christine's plump bottom.

All the men appeared ludicrous, with their pricks sticking up almost challenging their partners. Several of the women danced with their hands gripping or slowly pumping the members of their companions.

After a few spins, Arthur took Annie by her rump and raised her in the air. He continued to dance and at the same time he slipped his massive cock into her pussy. Without losing a step they continued to waltz, Arthur holding Annie by the buttocks so her cunt remained clamped over his cock.

"There's a good-looking couple for you." Lola indicated Arthur and Annie in their feverish embrace.

She didn't have a chance to elaborate on her opinion, for Stephen wheeled her to the floor (she was a bit too heavy to hoist in the air), bent her over and, after a few quick licks of her asshole, began to sodomize her on the spot. The others playfully called them obscene names.

Lola retained her excellent humour and chuckled with delight while she slid her long fingers along the back of Stephen's neck.

"No, Stevey darling, I want to finish this waltz. We are making a spectacle of ourselves in front of everyone."

However, the man would hear one of her useless pleading. He was right at the point of ramming his cock to the hilt inside her gorgeous asshole, when the door bell rang.

Everyone stopped dancing. They all looked astonished, and perhaps more than one entertained the thought of the police.

"At this hour? What in the world do people think? That they can break a party at any time?" Arthur appeared angry.

"Don't open the door, Arthur. It may be... and, oh, if my mother ever found out."

Linda fidgeted in her new fear. Lola took advantage of the occasion and freed herself from Stephen's clutches.

"I know who it is," she confessed to everyone. They all seemed to be greatly relieved.

"You're not going to open the door completely nude, Lola. You're out of your head." Nick warned.

The others waited without saying a word. They were all expecting a scene of some sort and showed their apprehension by shuffling about aimlessly.

Lola opened the door and called to whoever was outside.

"Oh, there you are. Finally. You know, you haven't come too soon. It is terribly late."

A young lad, who couldn't have been more than twelve years of age, entered timidly. He was dressed in country attire and he gazed at the naked women with hungry eyes bulging.

He gathered up enough courage to move a few steps toward the centre of the room. Then he became aware of the unusual setting and stepped back.

"Oh... I... I..."

"Don't be afraid, little one. We aren't going to eat you alive. Now have you brought your friends?"

"Yes, they're outside..."

"We'll call them in. What are you waiting for? You can see that everyone has been impatiently staying up late for you." Lola winked at the group, who as yet had not caught on.

"Come on in..." The boy shouted.

"That's it. Tell them to hurry... Quickly... By the way. What is your name little fellow?"

"Gus, miss." He turned red all over.

The boy jumped out of the door and a few seconds later he came back dragging a cord.

"Whoa, there. Come on, Ben, come on Jos."

Everyone let out a nice round 'oh' when they saw the surprise. Two small donkeys appeared on the end of the cord that Gus held in his tiny hand.

Lola followed the young lad and his two 'friends' into the living room.

"Well, my friends. Here it is. The surprise I had in store for you."

"But what in the world?... What does it mean, Lola? It's some kind of a joke, isn't it?" Arthur tried to clarify matters.

"Here they are. Two little donkeys, Ben and Jos. Just as talented as they can be."

Lola took control of the evening with her imposing posture and laughing air.

"Where did you find them, Gus?" She stroked the boy's hair and he turned crimson once more. "My boss runs a small circus outside the city. He said I could have them for the night if I would feed them properly," Gus explained timidly.

Lola patted Ben on his hairy mane and then spun around to tell her listeners the story.

"I've known Gus for a few days now. He told me the secret about these two stubborn donkeys. You'll see that they aren't just ordinary donkeys, but that they come from the best society."

"And what may I ask is so extraordinary about those two mangy beasts?" Stephen let his curiosity get the better of him.

"Ben, it is true, is the one I prefer. He knows how to mount a lady with all the delicacy of his art. You should see the way he gets on top of Jos – who is incidentally a lady, and we should all call her Josette."

Lola gave Ben a big kiss.

"Josette knows how to interest men as well. Isn't that so, Gus dear?"

The lad looked down at his feet and couldn't respond from embarrassment.

Helen wrapped her arms around the youngster, and the warmth of her nude breasts in his face didn't help matters any.

The boy apparently loved it, but kept his head bobbing from side to side.

"He's a real cutey. I wander how big he is? In the raw, naturally."

Helen evidently found Gus to her taste.

Annie detached herself from Arthur and skipped over to the two small animals.

"But what about that famous dick everyone talks so much about? How is it supposed to appear?"

"Some patience, sweetie." Lola wagged her finger at the impetuous teenager.

Lola took Ben and Josette by the cord and led them to the very centre of the room.

"Annie, you are going to suck Ben here. But will you remember that he is a donkey and not a man?"

"You'll see how I can make anyone sit up and take notice. Just let me at him."

Lola lifted her hand and pushed the girl back for a second.

"No. We will have our pleasure, make no mistake about that. But first of all, we should have some consideration for our guest of honour. Ben is prepared to shoot off at least a dozen times. I think we should start the fun off by giving him to..."

Everyone turned around and practically shouted in chorus: "Linda!"

"Who, me?" cried the girl.

"Bravo! A better choice could not have been proposed. You have my blessing, my lucky niece." Arthur led her over to Ben as though she were some charming princess being betrothed to her dashing prince.

"Just think of it – my niece shall be buttfucked by a donkey in front of my very eyes. Now *this* is what I should like to see when we get together. Thank you Lola, for your pleasant surprise. I hope *all* of you will come up with a little something before summer is over. Just a little imagination, that's all it takes."

Arthur was extremely happy. In fact, he went back to his desk and started to take notes.

During the little respite, Helen took Gus over to the divan. The big brunette was noted for her love of initiating newcomers to the clan. The lad let himself be had with his mouth wide open.

"Come on, sonny. Take off your clothes."

"Take off my clothes?"

"Of course. Do you wish me to help you...?"

And before Gus had a chance to say yea or nay, Helen was helping him off with his shirt. Soon he was completely nude. He was slightly built, but quite sturdy for his age. Between his thighs, which lacked the first signs of hair, stood his little prick. It wasn't all that small, and Helen was surprised to see the proportions of such a young and innocent-looking lad.

Helen began to tickle the youngster's balls with an air of avid concentration.

"Tell me, honey. Haven't you ever licked off a woman before?"

Gus looked up at her completely abashed. He swallowed and failed to respond.

Finally a few words squeaked out of his heart-shaped mouth.

"No. Honestly, I never have."

Helen was delighted to see her young lover squirm as though he were at the dentist waiting to get his tooth pulled.

"Well, I imagine that you haven't. If you had, you would have been unfaithful to me. And you would not want to be unfaithful to this pretty thing, would you?"

She led the boy's right hand down to her pussy and he nervously fingered the wet lips.

"No, ma'am."

Suddenly, with one brisk movement, Helen took the lad by the scruff of his neck and buried his face in her cunt.

"Go on, Gussy. Pretend it's ice cream. You like ice cream, don't you?"

Perhaps the suggestion registered, because Helen had her mouth agape with pleasure in no time.

"Oh, the little devil..."

Judging from Helen's reactions, Gus must have learned his lessons quickly. Helen, of course, was turned on by thinking of the fresh virgin she had between her legs.

But the grand spectacle was in the centre of the room, around the two donkeys. Linda, who had refused, conceded her turn to Annie.

The little glutton wasted little time in getting underneath the animal. She licked his belly and then pressed her hungry mouth against the animal's genitals.

In a few seconds the animal's pizzle popped out, red and powerful.

Annie continued to lick it while she took it in her two hands because of its enormous size.

"It's enormous," Christine confirmed.

"It's beautiful." Alice seconded the notion.

Linda was speechless. She just thought of the moment that it would bludgeon in her like a flagpole. It was going to be bad enough just accepting its size in her pussy, but how in the world would she take it in her butt? He would certainly rip her open.

"We'd better prepare Linda. She looks as though she is ready to pass out," Nick told the fellows close at hand.

"Afraid? Cut it out. Why, I'll bet the little bitch is as wet as a ditch just thinking of that engine pounding into her. Am I not right, Linda sweet? I'll bet you want that beast all over you. Confess honey, we're all behind you."

"No, no. I don't want him. He's too big!"

Lola came to her side and comforted the shaking girl by placing a friendly arm around her shoulder.

"Now, now, my love. It'll be marvellous."

"By the way, Lola, have you had the pleasure of tasting this lovely animal and receiving it in the you know where?" It was Stephen who asked.

Lola smiled with her famous superior air.

"Of course. Do you think I would subject my friend to such a thing if I had not attempted it myself? Ben is just great, and I advise that some of the men present take notice of his efforts. They will learn a good deal, believe me."

"Don't tell us that it was Gus that helped you in your... efforts, my dear?" Helen was writhing under the caresses of little Gussy.

"No, my darling, it was his boss. The man is Italian – and well you know the rest."

"Alright girls, don't fight. It's not worth the trouble. If you want to have it out over Benjamin later, then we can get the whips out and fight it tooth and nail."

Arthur had a way of settling all arguments tactfully. The two women had become catty over their prized possessions.

Nick was curious, and continued to bombard Lola with questions.

"And the boss participated, eh?"

"Alright, wise guy. I'll tell you what you want to know. We started off by having Ben do it cuntwise and his owner, Emmanuel, doing it from the rear. Then he got the dreadful – but wonderful – idea of having Benny stick it in my butt. I coolly accepted the proposition, while Emmanuel permitted himself to be sucked off. I might add that an agreeable time was had by all."

"I'll bet," Edgar snickered.

"That Italian is six-four and as strong as Hercules. I'm not sure who is the bigger, Benny or Emmy. And you can judge from the size of our tail-wagging friend that Emmanuel must have been somebody. I still can remember when he tossed me on the floor and said, 'Now both of us will slip in our bananas, my treasure.' Those were his exact words."

Lola was deep in a reverie, and she finally blinked her eyes and came out of it.

"Come on Linda, don't worry about a thing."

Linda stumbled over to Lola. The poor girl was shaking like a leaf. She still wasn't convinced. It was obvious she needed more than words to get her calm back.

"I ... just... can't."

Lola winked and once more calmed her down by telling her she would soon know what paradise was like. She showed the girl how to pass underneath the animal. She had her head right against that of the donkey with her arm around Ben's torso.

"Put your legs on the floor and keep your knees wide apart. Don't worry about a think, we'll take care of the rest."

Linda obeyed and remained in the indicated position. She could feel the strength of the little mule, and the musky odour of its genitals washed over her.

Suddenly she felt a veritable snake stiffen against her body. It was more than a cock. It was a baseball bat.

"My gosh. It really is huge," Nick remarked. "Do you think she will be able to take it?"

"She'll take it alright, and what's more she is going to love it. Just wait and see if I'm not right."

Lola took Benny's great pizzle and lodged it at Linda's orifice. The young girl jumped back at the contact.

"Ah, then you feel it?"

"And how," said Linda.

The animal, which before seemed to be indifferent to the whole thing, gave a leap forward as though he were impetuous and wished to enter the girl. The end of his pizzle gouged at her pussy and it made Linda cry out with a frightened howl.

"I think we need some vaseline." Lola signalled to Robert to go up to the bathroom for some of the lubricant.

Robert scampered back in no time, and Lola smeared great swathes of it over Linda's cunt-lips and then deep inside her pussy.

"Now that should do it. Ready Linda honey?"

"I'm all set," the girl retorted, really not at all sure of herself.

Everyone was down on his or her hands and knees to watch the penetration. Annie was getting the biggest thrill out of it, and she masturbated without letting up.

"Go to it, Benjamin old fellow," Arthur cried, chewing on his pipe. "Let her have it."

Lola put the prick back in position and the donkey, used to this sort of situation, pushed forward. This time his pizzle disappeared, inch by inch, into Linda's swollen pussy and up into her womb. Her eyes opened wide and she wanted to ask if she had not been ripped apart.

Instinctively she spread her legs wide apart to ride the blows. Already she wasn't thinking of avoiding the huge member, but instead she made every effort to facilitate matters, raising her buttocks off the ground and thrusting forward with hips grinding.

Everyone watched Linda as though they were hypnotised. The young teenager had been a virgin just a few days ago, yet now she was being raped by a donkey. It was like a dream. And for Linda it was a dream come true.

Uncle Arthur began to take notes. He carefully steadied himself on his knees as he wrote furiously on his ink pad.

Annie approached Ben with her tongue outstretched. She was dying to lick the donkey's balls.

Lola aided Linda by pushing her into a more favourable position.

"He's a doll, isn't he Linda honey? Let him get all the way in and you'll see what he's capable of."

"He wants to ride on top. It's no fun unless we can really help Linda to the heights of pleasure," commented Alice.

"I don't think I can stand any more of it," gasped Linda.

All at once she turned white. "He's going to kill me!"

Annie began to lick the frustrated beast's balls. This caused Benjamin to wiggle his prick further into Linda. A few drops of blood fell to the floor, showing that the mule had penetrated deep inside her.

Soon Linda's thighs were covered with streaks of blood. Ben started to let out a thunderous animal cry, and everyone guessed that he had spurted. But Lola insisted that the donkey was just getting to like the sport. Then he began to snort and buck, as though he were on the verge of a great orgasm. And lo and behold – he was. His thick donkey sperm flooded the near-unconscious girl's cunt and womb.

It was Lola who came to her rescue. The bronzed beauty dragged her backwards, disimpaling her. The bloody sperm left its thick trace on the carpet as it dropped in gouts from Linda's gaping pussy. Linda's stomach was spasming back and forth as she expelled the last drips of spunk out of her entrails.

"Now *that* was something. Lola, you're a genius. How did you ever think of it?" Stephen scratched his head.

Someone interrupted with a shout. It was Helen, who was right in the middle of a gigantic rousing orgasm brought on by the twinkling head of little Gus.

It was easy to see that Gus was excited about his position, because his little prick stuck up proudly, its tip leaking clear fluid, all the while his face was buried between Helen's tightly crossed thighs.

"Just look at that, will you. That bitch Helen couldn't wait to get hold of the little tyke. It's just like her to be greedy for newcomers." Arthur let his comments be heard by all, and in particular by Helen, who tossed it off lightly.

Christine threw an ironic smile over toward Gus and Helen, who were going through the final strains of their cunt-sucking lesson.

"And I thought he was a virgin," she exclaimed.

Once Helen had attained her pleasure, she raised the boy and up hugged him to her breasts. She permitted him to taste her cherry nipples. It was the kind of nibble the youngster richly enjoyed. He no longer remained timid. Gus bit into the teats as though they were made of cream cake.

Helen then cradled his prick in her fist, slowly pulling his wet foreskin back and forth over the glans, and the little fellow slobbered gluttonously over her nipples.

"Of course he is still a virgin. He's much too young to be otherwise. But *I'm* the one that is going to take it away from him and give him something else in exchange. After all, you've all amused yourselves with the donkey!"

She fondled Gus's head as though he were the most skilful of lovers.

"Don't be so possessive Helen. Wouldn't you like to feel Benjamin in you? I guess you prefer children's pencils to the crowbars of beasts."

Everyone laughed, and that included Helen. But she didn't let go of her boyish lover.

"Go on have your fun. While waiting my turn, I choose to

remain with Gussy and teach him some things. None of you are against my plans, are you?"

Helen looked pleased with herself.

"I'll start with the pencil and wind up with the crowbar in due course."

They all nodded their approval. Now, another candidate was needed for the donkey's prick. Annie and Christine were very impatient, and it was finally the youngest who got into the act.

Annie had much more experience than Linda, and she rapidly got into the desired position. Instead of the vaseline, Annie was licked out properly by Alice, while Christine moistened Ben by sucking on the end of his great pizzle. She had quite a time with the sperm that still trickled around the beast's balls.

"It's delicious. I've never tasted anything like it. Look how hard he is getting already."

"Hurry up and get him inside me. I'm awfully hot and I want him badly," Annie squealed.

Linda watched attentively. She lay on the carpet leaning on an elbow, observing the scene. She realized that the pain she had endured was only secondary to the pleasure. When she felt her crotch, she gathered up her own come mixed with Benny's ejaculation and some drops of blood. The act had been savage, but she appreciated the marvellous after-effects. She scolded herself for not having behaved better.

Now Annie was possessing that wonderful prick that only a few minutes ago had stuffed to the core her with its animal heat and immensity. She was proud that Benjamin had come inside her with all his donkey fury.

Alice and Christine continued to lick the beast's testicles. They soon managed to get his pizzle in perfect working order for feverish Annie. The teenager was spread apart impatiently, wiggling and begging for the enormous prick to split her.

"Come on now, damn it. Let me have it. I know how to manage him. I'll do it by myself."

She flew onto the great pole of flesh like an acrobat, deeply impaling herself. An outsider would have said that she had done it many times before with Benjamin. At the first penetration, Annie flinched with pain and let out a sharp raspy cry.

Ben had entered with a kick and was stuck fast in the

forefront of the youngster's pussy.

"Oh, it's great. I've never had anything like it between my legs. It hurts, but what the hell. It's terrific... but sensational... Go it, Benny, darling!"

Annie moved around like a fish out of water. She had Benjamin almost leaping in the air. Inch by inch the donkey penetrated her. Then, Annie started to shudder with noisy gasps and moans,

"Oh, oh... I feel it... coming... I want to come with him..."

It was almost as though the donkey had known what she desired. Benjamin began to bray and kick up his hind legs as though he wanted to dig in deeper. He started to shake and buck as if struck on the head. All at once he let loose. A stream of thick white cream shot into Annie's pussy. She rolled into him, trying to milk every last pearl of the sacred juice.

Then the girl crumpled to the ground, completely exhausted. She had a happy smile on her face.

"Hey, I'm next." Christine made her presence known to all.

"Let Benny have a rest," Stephen pleaded on behalf of the poor beast. "After all, he's not a machine. He's a genuine screwer like us, and he needs a rest once in awhile."

"He'll be able to rest up after I get through with him. I have a way with animals you know," Christine bragged.

Christine bent down to suck the dripping, half-hard pizzle. Although it was slightly soft, it retained its sizeable proportions. Christine took the prick in her mouth and rolled her tongue around it, cleaning off the blood and come.

She sucked avidly on the gobbets of sperm and washed the animal out with deliberate skill to make him hard again.

During Benjamin's star turn, the men in the room found that their activity had dropped off suddenly.

Arthur approached Josette and tapped her on the rear. The little she-donkey looked at him.

"I've tried everything else. This little bitch of a donkey has love in her eyes. I think I'll rip into her behind. It will do me good and I can chalk up another pleasure in my carnet."

Edgar, Stephen and Nick gathered around to watch this daring exploit.

"Why not? The girls are going wild over Benjamin. We

should have our share of fun with Josie here."

"And I'm new at this type of game. I've got to admit it fellows, I've never buttfucked a mule before," said Nick.

"I did it to a goat once." Arthur revealed his intimate secrets. "It was a few years back, while I lived in the mountains. I was with three friends. During a walk we met a splendid little creature, a white goat. It was tied to a tree. All three of us screwed her. It was an amusing experience."

Edgar approached Josette and pressed his cock, which had grown remarkably rigid, up to her flank. The beast did not budge. She was evidently used to such attentions.

"In order to penetrate with some ease, I think it would be better to stick on a little vaseline. Josette's anus appears awfully small."

"I think you're right, old chap. She seems as tight as a virgin. Better try some."

Arthur helped Edgar lubricate his cock. Once again Edgar aimed his weapon at Josie's asshole. This time the great head of his prick entered without any difficulty.

"How is it?" Alice asked as she approached the group.

"It's hot as a furnace," Edgar replied.

He moved about trying to get a deeper penetration. He then began a to and fro movement.

"Is she better than mine?" Alice asked in a sweet tone, obviously trying to gain a comparison.

Edgar didn't answer her. He was too busy giving Josette his best strokes. The man sighed away as though he had never tasted a similar treat. And in fact, Edgar, with all his earthly experience, had not.

Alice wanted to watch the achievement close-by. She decided to lap her tongue around the rim of Edgar's anus. Good-naturedly she went to work, pulling his buttocks apart so she could get her tongue right inside his sphincter, which was already oiled with the musky sweat of his exertions.

On the other side of the room Christine had Benjamin in a fine state. The animal was foaming at the mouth and it was apparent that he preferred Christine to the others. Christine was right when she told everybody she knew how to handle the animal.

She kept talking to Benny as though she had made love to

him all her life. Christine played with his balls while she hypnotised him with her feverish eyes.

"Maybe he just likes blondes," shrugged Stephen, trying to find a reason for her success.

Christine kept telling her friends of the marvellous effects. Arthur ran back to his desk and started taking notes.

The girl tried to open Ben's mouth and deep-kiss him, but the mule wouldn't have anything to do with her.

"He'll only French kiss with Josette, Christine. After all, the two are quite attached you know," Nick teased.

"He'll forget all about her when I get through. Look at the fire I've stirred in him already."

"You're going to look rather silly walking down the street with a donkey as your lover, dear," Nick jibed once again.

"The dirty beast. He wants to gouge my stomach out. I can feel his cock hammering in me like a steamshovel. What a monstrous prick this one has... Oh how it burns... It's like a bar of fire... When he trembles inside, there isn't a man living who can thrill me like that. This little donkey is... a real satyr, believe me."

Christine pressed herself up to the little donkey as though she were clinging to him for life, forcing her pussy further over his pizzle. She rubbed her lovely breasts against the skin of the beast. And all present could have sworn that Ben got hotter by this passionate treatment.

Christine must have come more than once, because she was panting like an exhausted sprinter. Her thighs were covered with her cunt-juice mixed with the donkey's own discharge.

"Since I've had someone like Benjamin, I can't settle for anything less. I'll go to any lengths to have something like this. Oh, it's good... but *really* good."

The others looked on and listened, surprised and admiring at the same time. Christine didn't put on any brakes in her exhibition. She let her real, sexual self come out and take charge.

Meanwhile, Helen was avidly teaching young Gus the techniques of expert love-making. The little fellow had his cock in her anus and was pumping away with mad frenzy.

In the meantime his mistress turned to talk to him as he plunged in and out of her tight asshole.

"Do you like that, Gus, honey? Are you about to come,

kiddo?"

Gus couldn't answer back. His emotions had gotten the better part of him and he was swallowing all the wind he could muster in order to hold on. There was no doubt that he was feeling something that he had never known before.

The atmosphere of the surprise reunion was getting into full swing. Christine had hardly time to be released from the fidgeting donkey when Lola started to suck Ben's red dick. Lola wanted the beast now and she took an aggressive action in showing just how much she desired him.

The men in the room were overwhelmed by the sudden sensation of desire and abandon. They were partly mad at the women for their over-attention of a mere mule. They decided to get even by taking some healthy whacks at Josette.

When Josette proved what she could do, the men soon forgot all about the women and concentrated on the delightful animal.

Nick had already come three times and was trying to fight off the others in an attempt to stick it out for a fourth.

Once the girls became aware that they had been abandoned, in true female fashion they hovered over the males to try to lure them away from the wondrous beast. It was just too evident that they were jealous of Josette.

The donkey glared at them haughtily. When Ben saw that things weren't going the way they should and his Josette was bored with mere mortal sex, he four-legged it over to his whinnying companion.

Nick stepped aside and permitted Benjamin to show the men just how Josie liked her sex.

The two animals went at it hammer and tongs. It aroused everyone, and Lola soon found that she was being buttfucked by Stephen.

Nick dropped Linda on her back, whipped her legs right over her shoulders and drove his red, swollen cock deep inside her succulent anus.

"You liked what you got from that crazy donkey. Well here's something else you won't forget." Nick pushed into her right up to his balls. Linda didn't utter a solitary cry. She liked it and wasn't in the least bit afraid of anything now.

Ben's gigantic phallus had opened new vistas for the girl.

Uncle Arthur was sucking Helen's tits at the same time she was preoccupying herself with Gus. Arthur was somewhat jealous, and he was finally forced to give the youngster a swift kick in the backside to dislodge him from Helen's rectum. Arthur then jumped on the beautiful brunette and scolded her.

"Aren't you getting tired of dicks the size of little fingers? Here, try a thumb for a change."

Helen began to laugh uproariously.

"You're talking about Benjamin I suppose. You aren't going to compare yourself to him, are you?"

Everyone was in a gay and playful mood by now. Annie had Edgar on her shoulders and Stephen was busy with Alice, and the maid, at the same time, was sucking off Robert.

Little Gus remained in the corner sheepishly while Arthur fucked the daylights out of Helen.

Lola was the happiest of all. She was underneath Benjamin and taking his huge phallus in her pussy like a trouper. Nearby Linda was being sodomized by Nick.

There was a profound silence in the living room. The couples were on their last lap, slowly sighing into a limp drowsiness. The first to speak was Lola.

"The festival isn't over yet, folks. Let's refresh ourselves with some sandwiches and beer."

Annie and Alice went to the kitchen and prepared a snack for the group.

"Good idea Lola. I was beginning to get hungry," Edgar yawned.

"Why don't we play a game in the meantime?" Christine suggested. Everyone chimed in with his or her proposition.

Finally Lola piped up with something that appeared to fit the bill.

"I know a game that is rather amusing. You have to guess what I am thinking..."

"What do we have to guess?" Helen quizzed.

Lola smiled and then continued.

"It's not complicated. One of us will lie on the floor with her legs apart and her eyes covered with a scarf. Then she'll have to guess who is the man on top. If she's wrong, she'll have to suffer an atrocious whipping. I know some of you girls are dying for it though. If she's right, she gets a bonus."

"Not a bad idea," Edgar agreed.

"First of all let's eat. Then we'll begin." Uncle Arthur was very considerate of his guests.

Alice and Annie came in with a platter of food and drink. They even had something for Benjamin and Josette.

Lola hoisted her glass of beer and offered a toast.

"To everyone's sexual health."

They all gathered around Benjamin and poured beer down his throat, while the scandalous little Annie tried to suck him off once more. Benjamin responded by sending a great jet of piss down her throat, and she drank it all down as if it were lemonade.

Lola clapped her hands.

"Let's begin our game."

"Who is going to be first?"

"How about Linda?"

"I was sure of it," said Christine.

Linda didn't hesitate. She took the position her elders desired and she permitted her eyes to be covered by a perfumed handkerchief, which belonged to the voluptuous Lola.

Lola waved Stephen over. He knelt down and stuck his penis deep in the blindfolded girl's asshole.

"Who is it?"

"I'm not sure..," Linda responded.

"She's just doing that on purpose. Maybe she can't feel any more."

"Be quiet Annie, and give her a chance," Lola scolded.

Stephen warmed to the task, plunging his cock into Linda's already stretched anus. He pistoned in and out.

"Who is it?" Lola questioned.

"She's just putting on an act to get more, the little rascal."

Stephen dug his prick deeper into the luscious asshole, which felt as wet and warm as a pussy. He tried to keep from moaning his pleasure so as not to give himself away.

"Do you know who it is, Linda?" Lola questioned.

"No. Not yet... Let me feel him a little more..."

"But of course," Annie chimed in. She certainly was dying to be in Linda's place.

"She's just putting on the dog. The little whore couldn't ask for anything better."

Stephen now had his cock deeply embedded in Linda's rear and he started to poke her brutally. The girl, mistaken as to the width of the member, shouted out in a raspy half-happy, half-painful voice.

"It's Edgar, isn't it?... Edgar?"

The others were gleeful to see that she was wrong. Linda would have to pay the price of sucking each and every one of them.

"No, take a look. It isn't Edgar. It's Stephen. You'll have to pay the penitence, dear."

Arthur was wondering whether his niece did this on purpose. He questioned whether she was that vicious. Perhaps she really was gifted with the libertine family traits.

Stephen was forced to give up his masterful performance. He wanted to finish what he had started but he was out-numbered and had to abide to the rules of the game.

"Let me be the first," Nick piped up.

"No, first of all she is going to lick out all the women. And then suck their assholes... And then after..."

"And then after?" Annie's eyes were as big as stars.

"Then she will have the unique pleasure of being sodomized by Benjamin."

Everyone applauded Lola's brilliant proposition. They all imagined the immense delight that was awaiting them. The women lined up. Annie and Christine, naturally, were the first to proffer their wet snatches.

"She better give her all, or she'll see what I'm capable of."

The warning came from Christine.

Linda knelt down before the excitable Christine, who dug her fingernails into Linda's scalp and forced her head into her bush.

"Get in there and suck, sweetie. Do a good job, or it'll be the whip."

Christine had a reputation for not playing around. Crisp and cool, she needled Linda into a frenzy. Soon Linda was slobbering in the soaking folds Christine's pussy.

Annie jumped into the game as soon as she saw that Christine was on the verge of coming.

"Damn you, get back before I thrash you. I haven't come yeeeeeettt..." Due to the adroit licking tongue of the schoolgirl eating her pussy, Christine barely managed to finish her sentence. And at that, it was on a very high note.

After Annie, who tried to come twice after concealing her first orgasm, Helen almost suffocated the poor little dear.

Alice made Linda work very hard. The skimpy maid was terribly blasé over the whole thing, acting like a royal duchess. Her cunt still reeked of cheap perfume and come.

Real love was demonstrated with Lola however. Linda stuck her finger up Lola's behind and then put the finger in her mouth to mix the two, the come and the shit, to induce a real sensual pleasure. Both girls sucked the mixture, and Linda kept her finger embedded in Lola's asshole while she licked her clit until she came.

Once the women were content, everyone flocked around Benjamin. He and Linda were the star for that night. Arthur promised everyone a repeat performance some other time.

Nick took one of Ben's front legs and Robert the other. They lifted the beast in the air, while Linda sat on her knees. Lola informed her things would go better if she would put her buttocks high in the air. The girl listened attentively and had enough confidence in Lola to heed her warning.

Once Linda's pink, dilated asshole waggled in front of Benjamin's slow-growing prick, Helen took hold of it by the root and aimed it at Linda's orifice. The odour coming from her orifice inflamed the beast, and he rammed his pizzle home. Linda yelled like a martyr. Yet she held fast, and once the donkey's prick was fully up her asshole and the worst of the pain subsided, she began to relax and appreciate the fantastic sensation.

The mere thought of having such a tremendous organ in her bowels made Linda proud, not to mention turned on, and she was in form to give everyone what they came for.

The girl bucked and ground her hips like the best of professional belly dancers, only she was presenting her asshole. Her glistening sphincter, stretched to near bursting, cinched around the root of Ben's pizzle, milking the first drops of hot come from his balls.

Benjamin was delighted. He let out a few 'hee-haws' that gave all a few laughs. The mule kept driving home in Linda's boiling asshole.

"This is one of the better shows you've put on Arthur, my lad. Continue the good work," enthused Edgar.

It wasn't long before Benjamin rammed his cock in so far that Linda froze halfway in the air. "Ahhhhhhhh!" The girl cried as a golden smile crept over her lips.

Linda had reached a divine climax, but still the donkey rammed home. Christine came to the rescue by sucking on Ben's balls.

The animal's voice grew harsh and hoarse. Then with a bellowing, rough cry he let out his explosion. Linda was shot forward as though she were being fired from a cannon. Christine was pinned underneath the hind legs, which had given away.

Everyone applauded.

"Bravo!" Nick and Helen shouted in unison.

Linda fell forward in a stupor as the donkey's prick slowly withdrew from her asshole in a spray of jism, blood and shit.

The party had reached its denouement successfully. The guests, as well as the hosts were content.

When the bunch left that evening after having another round of food and drinks, Arthur felt proud and placed his arm over Linda's shoulder. The girl was dog-tired. She smiled bravely and excused herself for being such a slouch at the beginning of the evening.

The gang hailed her as an excellent newcomer, and Nick invited her to his home for the get-together the following weekend.

Arthur heartily shook Edgar's hand and the friends patted each other on the back.

"You're a real champ, Arthur, believe me. Give the girls some more for me." Edgar waved goodbye as he parted with the rest of the sated, delighted guests.

epilogue

Late that night, Arthur came into Linda's room. His strange eyes grew grave and insisting. Though tired, Linda was happy to submit to her uncle's lust. She felt the hour was perfect, three in the morning, and that her uncle, with excellent taste, had wakened her in the middle of a most erotic dream.

The man violated the girl. He bit into her ear lobe, her calf, her behind. Arthur, completely thrown into a peculiar state of lust, sucked at the girl's pussy as though it were the remains of a dried lemon.

Linda was driven to passionate heights as she licked and sucked on Arthur's majestic prick. The two ransacked each other for the delights of the flesh, and it was evident that they had achieved a perfect unity.

Suddenly Arthur leaped up and put his thin fingers on Linda's shoulders.

"Linda. I believe I'm in love with you."

"But uncle, what about Lola? You have been with her for a good number of years. It wouldn't be fair to her. She is so fond of you."

Arthur tumbled out of bed quite naked. He began to rub his hips. The man was clearly bothered by the thought of Lola.

"Lola doesn't mean a thing to me now that you've come into my life. You are the perfect fuck. She will just have to resign herself to it. Besides, Lola doesn't care about anyone but herself. She is mad with lust and hasn't the slightest notion of what love might be."

Linda stretched her bruised side, still sore from the powerful grasps of her uncle.

"Uncle Arthur, isn't our relationship incestuous?"

"My dear little nymph. It has been from the beginning. The

only thing I hadn't counted on was my love for you. My love for Linda, the princess I wanted to create. Well, you're the creation. And I have become a luckless Pygmalion."

Uncle Arthur came back to the bed and took Linda's hand and placed it on his cock, which was half limp.

Uncle and niece gazed into each other's eyes and saw love. For Linda, it came as a shock. She couldn't really say whether she was truly in love with her uncle or not.

She was very, very fond of him, certainly. Her love for him was much more in the vein of respect for an elder, although she now had a craving for him sexually.

In her confusion, Linda placed her arms around Arthur's neck and squeezed tightly.

"Oh, uncle Arthur. I don't know how I feel really."

Uncle Arthur, still sitting close to the girl, pushed his stiff prick against the cunt-lips of his sweet, sentimental niece.

"This time, my dear, we are going to make love slowly and with... *feeling.*"

He slipped his cock into the schoolgirl's hot, hungry gash. She arched back and accepted the full length of the handsome organ.

Arthur's hand crawled up and down her spine and finally came to rest on her buttocks. He squeezed and then sighed.

"How I love your backside, darling." He stuck his finger in the crevice between her buttocks and tickled her asshole.

Linda put her long tongue deep inside her uncle's mouth. Their tongues entwined in delight and their salivas mixed together lasciviously.

They embraced for several minutes, unaware that the door to Linda's room was slightly ajar.

Arthur crushed the girl to him and his cock drilled into her pussy.

"Can't you feel me, dear. I'm as hard as a rock. I want to last a lifetime with you. Buck a little, Linda, and show me your grace."

The girl obeyed and demonstrated her talent as a fully-fledged lover, her movements drawing him nearer to climax. Suddenly the door burst open and Lola, red-eyed and with her hair mussed and agitated, strode into the room.

In her hand she brandished a horse-whip. Lola had fire in her eyes. Her hand nervously gripped the ugly weapon.

"So Arthur. This is what you plan on doing to me. No more shall we pass the small hours of the morning making love. You've found someone else. A girl who passed as a friend at first, and now look at her. A tramp. Well, I'll get my vengeance."

She let the whip crack at the bed-post. It made such a loud crack that Linda had to blink from the noise it made.

"The donkey wasn't enough for you was it Linda? Well maybe we can give the evening some variety yet."

A wicked blow caught the girl around the neck and almost strangled her. When Arthur got up to protest, he was met with a vicious whip-lash that got him around the mid-section. The man doubled up in pain.

"Lola, you... you've gone out of your mind. What are you trying to prove?" The man spoke in pain.

Another sting of the lash caught him directly on the back and took the wind out of him for several seconds.

"Go ahead Arthur. Suffer a bit. It will do you good. You've been the great lord here. Everything you wanted was placed at your feet. How does it feel to get a taste of your own medicine?"

Lola swiped the whip down on the man's left foot. He yelped like a dog writhing in pain.

Linda came to the protection of her uncle. But she was met with a rain of blows that cut into her breasts and buttocks. Lola was trying to drive the whip into her asshole.

"Lola, put down that whip or I'll never forgive you. You've lost your head." Arthur just managed to puff these words out. He fought to regain his breath.

For a moment Lola hesitated. She knew Arthur's wrath, but this time she was definitely going to face it all the way. The tigress was determined to fight her man to the last breath.

By a glance of daggers, the two former lovers declared war. Linda began to whimper. For the first time since her visit to the villa, she became afraid, truly afraid.

With back-swipes and overhand blows, Lola let fly with that horrible lash. Instead of seeking cover, Arthur crawled toward her. He had the disadvantage of having the frightened Linda clinging to him like a leech.

"Wiggle on the carpet with your princess, you worm. I'll have you both as striped as bloody zebras!"

Linda bit her lip and when she cried the pain caused by an excess of breathing made her dig her nails into her uncle's torso. Arthur struggled to get to his feet and stumble forth in search of the whip. He tried to ward off the blows with his elbow, but to no avail.

Within a few minutes, Lola had them both bleeding. Arthur bled from the mouth as though he had suffered internally. His back was streaked with red bruises. Linda matched him with her stripped, blood-flecked body.

"Now, you know what it is like to cheat your mistress."

Lola's eyes were like two red flames. Linda had never seen the bewitching woman in such a state of emotion as this before.

"You'll remember me Linda, won't you? Especially when you make true love to that bruised, beaten body."

Lola, who had her back up against the door, was suddenly thrown forward when the door was pushed open by Robert.

"Grab her, Robert boy."

Robert, realizing that a scandalous fight was taking place, obeyed his uncle and locked the woman's arms to her side. This gave Arthur a sufficient amount of time to stagger over to the furious whip-wielder.

With his remaining strength he slapped her across her proud and aggressive face. His next move was to snatch the whip from her hands. Arthur threw the weapon to the far corner of the room.

He met the defiant eyes with a backslap that caused Lola's head to bob up and down. Her eyes returned to meet his. Linda was surprised to see how brazen her friend was. Linda still felt that the rude intrusion was just a bad dream. But when she rubbed her tender bottom, she was quickly restored to reality.

"Now Lola, it's my turn to get even. And you know when I get angry, it isn't very much fun."

Uncle Arthur meant business. He signalled to Robert to come close for instructions.

"They've all gone home by now, I suppose. We let Gus sleep with his donkeys in the garage. Robert, I want you to go down and get Benjamin. We haven't finished with the little mule yet. Our dear Lola is going to find out what Benny's really like."

Arthur let out a cruel laugh that slightly took Lola aback. Even Linda tried to plead with her vengeful uncle.

"Don't you think she has suffered enough for the evening? I'm sure she'll apologize and then everything will be alright. Please, uncle Arthur."

"No, Linda. I have no intention of letting her get off so easily. She must learn a lesson, here and now."

Arthur ripped off Lola's pyjamas and twisted her left nipple. Lola just gritted her teeth without uttering a cry. Arthur slapped her across the mouth.

"You are a proud bitch aren't you? Well, I've got a new mistress now and you will serve me in the most docile way. I'll tame you, my ex-darling."

Arthur put his hand to his chin trying to think of a million and one tortures to bestow upon the hapless brunette.

All at once Lola ran over to Linda and clutched her arm. She spoke to the girl in a terribly intense voice.

"Can't you see how he is? He will treat you like dirt one day and cast you aside. Think what you are doing, Linda. You will only be a princess for a short while, and then he'll give you up as he is doing with me."

Linda felt that Lola was right, but she could do nothing about it for the moment. She was surprised to see that Arthur was paying little attention to them. He was apparently lost in his own thoughts of cruel vengeance.

"Linda, go to my room and in my blue dress on the bed you'll find the keys to the car. Put on any clothes you can find and leave this terrible place."

Linda was pushed to the door. Without any hesitation she ran to Lola's room. Uneven in her thoughts, she questioned herself as to whether she was doing the right thing.

Once in Lola's room she searched for the keys and found them in the blue dress. Then she went over to the wardrobe and grabbed a rose dress and a heavy overcoat.

As she was hurriedly putting on the dress, she heard some foot-steps behind her. She turned around startled and frightened. Arthur and Lola barred the doorway.

Linda was taken aback at the sight of the two together.

They had evidently patched up their quarrel.

"So you want to leave me just like that, Linda? What, you prefer the cold night to your warm tender uncle?"

Linda was speechless. She gazed at Lola for help, but the tiger woman was indifferent and languidly smoked a cigarette.

"You fell into our trap, Linda. Arthur wanted to see how faithful you would be. We planned that sham together. You didn't suppose for a minute that Arthur and I would leave each other for a mere child, did you?"

Linda's mouth dropped wide open. Their ruse fell into place. *She* would be the one who would have to pay the terrible price. It was difficult to imagine the games those two adults were capable of playing.

Once again the door flew open and Robert entered, dragging the obstinate Benjamin. The donkey seemed thoroughly wide-awake for such a late hour.

"If you have eyes to see with, Linda honey, you will notice that Benjamin has just had a shit. Like all men animals, he has an asshole too. You will kindly step up and lick Ben there, and properly. If not, I assure you that the consequences will be tenfold."

Linda felt so helpless that she unthinkingly walked over to the animal and knelt so that her head bumped its flanks. Ben's furry balls swung in her face and he brayed horribly.

Arthur pushed her by the neck, and her nose almost stuck in the animal's rear-end. The odour was horrible and sickly. Linda swallowed to keep from throwing up.

"Alright Linda, now lick the shit out of Benny's asshole. It may be quite tasteful. You never know."

Linda, with tears streaming down her face, tongued delicately at the mule's behind. Benjamin had recently had a shit alright, and animals usually don't get a chance to wipe out their rears.

Soon Linda's mouth was encrusted with a brown sticky mess. Lola kicked the poor girl on the rump and goaded her on.

"Come on. You can do better than that. Benny has a disdainful look on his face."

Linda steeled herself and burrowed her tongue further into the slippery asshole. The odour was nauseating, but somehow it affected the girl's senses and she wound up by almost enjoying the

---

horrifying, but excitingly taboo, act.

"Well, well. I think she is winding up by liking Benjamin more and more. What do you say we adopt Benny for our household, Lola? We could always make good use of him. Needless to say, Linda would adore him."

The young girl turned crimson, and with the lumps of Ben's shit around her mouth, she looked quite a sight.

"I can't go on, uncle dear. Please, I'm feeling terrible."

"Just get some of the shit that dripped down along his legs. Then tongue him deeply and sincerely, and we will let you go. Have no fears about it, dear."

Linda did has she was told. She leaned down to the sturdy little hind quarters and lapped up some of the brown matter that had trickled there. Then she came back to the anus and tongued it as deeply as she could for a few minutes. She imagined it was the asshole of her lover, and towards the end of the second or third minute, Linda was so dazed with pleasure that Lola had a hard time dragging her away.

"Why the little bitch enjoys it. Look, she's coming. Just look at her thighs. They're covered with cunt-juice."

"What do you expect? After all, when I said she was my princess, I didn't mean to exaggerate. This girl is open to all callings. Why Lola, in no time we shall have her doing the most splendid sexual feats imaginable."

Linda was doing such a good job of cleaning out Benny's behind that the young mule had worked up an erection. He was helped along in his sexual urges by Linda's skilful manipulation of his balls. Her fine fingers worked from one testicle to the other.

"Go ahead, Lola. I see what you're after. You can get it all in your mouth – but open wide dear."

With great dexterity, Lola slid down under the animal and wielded the baseball bat-sized prick toward her hungry mouth. She slobbered it up. The force of the cock almost completely distorted her face. Lola inhaled deeply and sucked longingly on the gigantic pizzle.

"Uncle Arthur, can't I take Linda from the rear? She's just dying for it. Look at the way she is waggling around and dripping. Come on uncle, be nice."

It was true that Linda was giving someone the come-on

signal; her youthful buttocks were swinging from left to right and then slowly grinding in the humid air.

"Go to it, Robert. But you better knock it home. This girl is very, very special and we want to handle her with care."

Robert leaped on Linda's back and drove his twitching cock deep into her distended anus. This only caused the girl to bury her head deeper in Benny's behind.

Arthur wanted to take a picture for his archives. The setting was delightful and the scene was elegant. He mused and thought that if he did take a snapshot, nobody would ever believe it. They would think it was a posed shot. And yet it was happening, right there before him.

The good uncle felt his cock rampant and burning with lust. It was almost purple with feverish engorgement. Arthur rushed over to Lola and dragged her from the donkey's penis by the roots of her hair.

"Lola, work on this for a while."

While the donkey brayed its discontent, Lola gluttonously poured her saliva over Arthur's hot cock.

Robert plunged away into Linda's precious asshole, while the 'princess' licked out Ben's backside with the most professional of oral agility.

As Lola crouched in front of Arthur, sucking him with all her skill, he barked orders to Robert to step up his speed.

"You little wretch. Let her have it with your best punches, Robert. Why the devil can't you have any appreciation for female bodies? All you ever think of his shooting your load. I'll have to teach you a thing or three."

He bounded away from Lola, who spat out a few drops of burning come. She was taken aback to see the man rampage about without considering her ultimate pleasure.

Arthur pushed Robert away and straddled the behind of the fair Linda. His enormous cock ripped into her gaping asshole as she continued to lap clean the donkey.

"This is the way it is done, Robert fellow. Roll around a little. Then go in and out. And then... all the way in. Make it... really good and deep."

Linda attested to the effect of this brand of action. She groaned her pleasure like a she-wolf howling to the moon.

"Get it, Robert? In... all... the... way... and then out slowly. Then tickle her cunt-lips with the head of it. Don't you see how she backs into it for the sheer love of it?"

And, indeed, Linda was backing into Arthur's fat prick. She wiggled her behind into a perfect position and at the same time she never lost a stroke with her tongue. Benjamin was dripping his spunk onto the expensive carpet.

Lola came to his rescue and placed her insatiable mouth around the animal cock. She siphoned out the hot white liquid and her eyes rolled with a mad joy as she swallowed it by the pint.

In the meantime, Robert was so hot and excited that he had to masturbate. At the last moment he bounded upon Lola and exploded his rigid cock into the beauty's anus.

All four were having a ball, but the one who appeared to be enjoying it the most was Benjamin, the astounding donkey. His eyes closed and he must certainly have entered a real animal paradise. He drooled at the mouth and brayed his delight.

The heat that the four created could be seen by the condensation on the window pane. The odour of Ben in particular caused the foursome to devote their very best efforts to the action at hand.

Inside of a quarter of an hour, the bedroom stank of shit and ejaculations. But this did not stop the couples from going into their third or fourth orgasm.

"I swear that I love you, Linda my darling princess."

Linda didn't care whether her uncle was sincere or not. She just kept up the hip-pumping movements which were bringing her closer to another juice-spraying orgasm.

She turned from the donkey's rear-end and responded to her uncle's caresses.

"I love you too, Arthur."

"Then you'll be my princess for life. You'll wait on me hand and foot, and I'll lead you to the finest sexual thrills that can be had."

"Yes, uncle dear." Linda squinted with the joy of his fat prick plunging deeper and deeper into her.

From the floor, Lola agitated around the donkey's belly. She seemed annoyed with Robert.

"You're no damned good, you little stinker. You've come

twice already and every time it goes flat. I guess it's your age that makes you so impetuous. I prefer Benjamin to you, my dear boy, as much as I regret telling you this."

Robert didn't give a damn. His appetite was grand and he decided to make the best of a special occasion.

"Just think of what Annie, Nick and the others are missing. And Alice is fast asleep in her little nook. This is tremendous. I could go at it all night."

"Just don't try it. It will probably kill you. Let me alone with Benjamin. He is my true lover, since Arthur has left me limp and flat."

Linda heard these infamous words, and this time she wasn't deceived by the ruse. She really didn't give one drop of 'donkey shit' whether the woman was serious or not.

"Linda, promise me that you won't go back to school without my approval. After all, you've learned much more here with me – and just think what more is in store for you."

Linda was set back by this unfamiliar proposal. She still had two years to go. And it was true, however, that in the course of a few days she had learned more about 'life' that she could ever have picked up in school.

However, she wanted to go back and put her knowledge into practice. It was difficult to make a decision at such a crucial time. Arthur spread her legs wide apart and over his shoulders as he penetrated deeper than ever.

"I'll do whatever you think best, uncle dear. But don't you think my education will be neglected?"

"I'll get a tutor. I have just the one for you. He is known to be the finest lover in all of Europe. His name is Paul and he has a penis that is a foot long, no less. And it creates the strangest sensation inside, the women tell me."

At that moment Linda was consumed with a burning climax that coursed through every nerve of her body.

"Ahhhhhhh..."

The girl came and came. It was hard to tell whether it was due to her uncle or the mention of the name of a lover, Paul with the fabulous phallus.

Arthur pistoned into the girl with his most violent thrusts. He grew hotter and hotter as he felt the girl's discharge burn his

---

swollen prick.

"Now you've really excited me, Linda. I think that I too... am... comminnnnng!"

Arthur clenched his teeth. He turned suddenly white and his head dropped on Linda's left shoulder. The man had just released a veritable tidal wave of jism.

Benjamin brayed for the fifth time. And Lola received a flood of hot spunk in her gorgeous mouth. It poured out of the corners and dripped down her neck.

Robert renewed himself by masturbating frenetically, like a deranged monkey. He made another attempt to leap upon Lola, but she would have none of it.

Arthur, limp as a rag, tried to compose a sentence. But due to his fatigued state, he failed to find the right words. Suddenly he regained his senses. He fondled Linda's soft hair and bit her back.

"My princess..." he uttered weakly.

Linda had rolled away from Benjamin and fell lifeless on the carpet.

When she opened her eyes she saw Arthur leaning over her. He had a strange humble look in his eyes. Linda almost thought it was the look of love.

Then of all things, she witnessed a tear that rolled down her uncle's cheek. His eyes blurred and his mouth gently sucked her teats. Once he returned to the surface he met her stupefied glance.

With a flood of tender words he sang a hymn in her honour, then he slid down to her feet and kissed then passionately. First the right, and then the left.

Arthur stretched his tired body over his niece's belly. Once more he had grown stiff, and was searching for the hot young pussy that he so cherished.

"Oh Linda. Allow me to be your... your *prince*."

THE LUSTS OF THE LIBERTINES
The Marquis De Sade

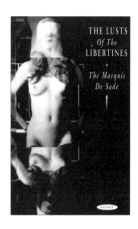

The Circle of Manias, the Circle of Excrement, the Circle of Blood; three gateways to a living Hell envisaged by the Marquis de Sade as he simmered in the bowels of the Bastille. An infernal zone where Libertines are free to pursue and execute their every caprice, no matter how depraved or inhuman.

Here, in a brand new, unexpurgated and explicit translation, are the 447 "complex, criminal and murderous lusts" of the Libertines as documented by de Sade in his accursed atrocity bible *The 120 Days Of Sodom;* a catalogue of debaucheries, cruelties and pathological perversions still unequalled in the annals of transgressive literature.

DUNGEON EVIDENCE: *Correct Sadist II*
Terence Sellers

The Mistress Angel Stern presides without mercy over a New York dungeon where her slaves, the "morally insane" of modern society, obey her every whim and undergo any degradation she wills upon them.

In the closed confines of a torture zone, these paraphiliacs and sexual malcontents use her image as an object for their masturbatory depravities, craving her cruelty in an abyss of sadomasochism and bondage.

Here are the bizarre case histories, philosophies and psychopathologies of a dominatrix; a frank testament which reveals not only the drives which lead some to become slaves, but also the complex exchange of psychic energies involved in scenes of dominance and submission.

THE VELVET UNDERGROUND
Michael Leigh

Swingers and swappers, strippers and streetwalkers, sadists, masochists, and sexual mavericks of every persuasion; all are documented in this legendary exposé of the diseased underbelly of '60s American society.

The Velvet Underground is the ground-breaking sexological study that lent its name to the seminal New York rock'n'roll group, whose songs were to mirror its themes of depravity and social malaise.

Welcome to the sexual twilight zone, where the death orgies of Altamont and Helter Skelter are just a bull-whip's kiss away.

SISTER MIDNIGHT *Jeremy Reed*

The Marquis de Sade is dead – but his sister is alive and well, stalking the ruins of the château of La Coste where she reconstructs the apocalyptic orgies, tortures and blasphemies of her brother's reviled last will and testament, *The 120 Days Of Sodom.*

Castle freaks, killing gardens, lesbian love trysts on human furniture; these and countless other configurations of debauched carnality conspire and collude in a sundered, dream-like zone where the clock strikes eternal midnight.

Sister Midnight is the sequel to Jeremy Reed's erotic classic *The Pleasure Château,* a continued exploration of decadent extremes and sexual delirium in the tradition of de Sade, Sacher-Masoch and Apollinaire; a tribute to undying lust and the endless scope of human perversion.

THE SNAKE *Melanie Desmoulins*

When Lucy, a sexually frustrated young widow, is mysteriously sent a plane ticket to Portugal, she takes a flight into erotic abandon which can only lead to death and damnation.

Soon seduced by both a debauched Englishwoman and her Portuguese husband, she sheds the skin of morality like a snake and begins to act out her darkest, uninhibited sexual desires. Increasingly depraved rituals of narcotics abuse, Satanism and sadomasochism – presided over by Bartolomeo, a Sade-like albino cult leader – eventually lead to the total disintegration of Lucy's ego.

At Bartolomeo's isolated villa, a shrine to pornographic art and literature, she finally enters the snake pit...

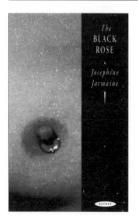

THE BLACK ROSE *Josephine Jarmaine*

Abducted to a mysterious French island, sixteen-year-old Rosamund finds herself at the mercy of the Duke and his four libidinous sons. She soon learns that her virginity must be sacrificed in order to breed the Black Rose, a rare flower whose aphrodisiac elixir will transform the world into a polysexual playground of orgiastic and orgasmic excess.

Rosamund's carnal initiation plunges her into a vortex of pain and pleasure, as she discovers that the Château Rose is a sensory realm where sadism, sapphism, sodomy, incest, bestiality, bondage and rampant fornication are a way of life.

The Black Rose is a stunning hybrid of decadence and explicit sexuality, a unique modern classic.

VELVET PUBLICATIONS

PHILOSOPHY IN THE BOUDOIR *The Marquis de Sade*

In the boudoir of a sequestered country house, a young virgin is ruthlessly schooled in evil. Indoctrinated by her amoral tutors in the ways of sexual perversion, fornication, murder, incest, atheism and complete self-gratification, she takes part with growing abandon in a series of violent erotic orgies which culminates with the flagellation and torture of her own mother – her final act of liberation.

Philosophy In The Boudoir is the most concise, representative text out of all the Marquis de Sade's works, containing his notorious doctrine of libertinage expounded in full, coupled with liberal doses of savage, unbridled eroticism, cruelty and violent sexuality. The renegade philosophies put forward here would later rank amongst the main cornerstones of André Breton's Surrealist manifesto.

THE SHE-DEVILS *Pierre Louÿs*

A mother and her three daughters...sharing their inexhaustible sexual favours between the same young man, each other, and anyone else who enters their web of depravity. From a chance encounter on the stairway with a voluptuous young girl, the narrator is drawn to become the plaything of four rapacious females, experiencing them all in various combinations of increasingly wild debauchery, until they one day vanish as mysteriously as they had appeared.

Described by Susan Sontag as one of the few works of the erotic imagination to deserve true literary status, *The She Devils (Trois Filles De Leur Mère)* remains Pierre Louÿs' most intense, claustrophobic work; a study of sexual obsession and mono-mania unsurpassed in its depictions of carnal excess, unbridled lust and limitless perversity.

THE PLEASURE CHATEAU *Jeremy Reed*

The story of Leanda, mistress of an opulent château, who tirelessly indulges her compulsion for sexual extremes, entertaining deviants, transsexuals and freaks in pursuit of the ultimate erotic experience. She is finally transported to a zone where sex transcends death, and existence becomes a never-ending orgy of the senses. The book also includes *Tales Of The Midget*, astonishing erotic adventures as related by a dwarf raconteur versed in decades of debauch.

Jeremy Reed, hailed as one of the greatest poets of his generation, has turned his exquisite imagination to producing this masterpiece of gothic erotica in the tradition of de Sade, Apollinaire and Sacher-Masoch, his tribute to the undying flame of human sexuality.

FLESH UNLIMITED *Guillaume Apollinaire*

The debauched aristocrat Mony Vibescu and a circle of fellow sybarites blaze a trail of uncontrollable lust, cruelty and depravity across the streets of Europe. A young man reminisces his sexual awakening at the hands of his aunt, his sister and their friends as he is irremediably corrupted in a season of carnal excess.

Flesh Unlimited is a compendium edition of *Les Onze Mille Verges* and *Les Mémoires d'Un Jeune Don Juan*, Apollinaire's two wild masterpieces of the explicit erotic imagination, works which compare with the best of the Marquis de Sade.

Presented in brand new translations by Alexis Lykiard (translator of Lautréamont's *Maldoror*), these are the original, complete and unexpurgated versions, with full introduction and notes.

THE WHIP ANGELS *Anonymous*

Victoria's journal reveals her darkest secrets, her induction into a bizarre yet addictive sexual underground at the hands of her immoral, incestuous guardians. Behind the façade of everyday life seethes black leather mayhem, voluptuous eruptions of demonic angels from timeless torture zones, a midnight twist heralded by the bullwhip's crack and the bittersweet swipe of the cat.

Blazing with erotic excess and incandescent cruelty, *The Whip Angels* is a feast of dominance and submission, of corrupted innocence and tainted love. In the tradition of *The Story Of O* and *The Image*, this modern classic was written by an anonymous French authoress (believed to the wife of Georges Bataille) fully versed in the ways of whipcord and the dark delirium of those in both physical and spiritual bondage.

HOUSE OF PAIN *Pan Pantziarka*

When a young streetwalker is picked up by an enigmatic older woman, she finds herself launched on an odyssey of pleasure and pain beyond measure. Lost in a night world, thrown to the lusts of her anonymous captors, she must submit to their increasingly bizarre rituals of pain and degradation in order to embrace salvation.

House Of Pain is scorched earth erotica, an unprecedented glimpse of living Hell, the torments and raptures of a young woman abandoned to the throes of rage, violence and cruelty which feed the sexual impulse. Churches, hospitals, courtrooms, all become mere facets of the same unyielding edifice, a bedlam of desire and flesh in flame beneath the cold black sun of her own unlimited yearnings.

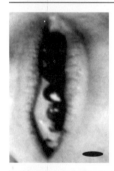

IRENE'S CUNT *Louis Aragon*

First published in France in 1928, *Le Con d'Irène ("Irene's Cunt")* is the last lost masterpiece of Surrealist Erotica. The author of this enigmatic and scandalous work is now known to be the great Surrealist Louis Aragon. Like Georges Bataille's *Story Of The Eye*, written the same year, *Irene's Cunt* is an intensely poetic account, the story of a man's torment when he becomes fixated upon the genitalia of an imaginary woman and is reduced to voyeuristically scoping 'her' erotic encounters.

In between describing various events in brothels and other sexual adventures, Aragon charts an inner monologue which is often reminiscent of Lautréamont, and of Artaud in its evocation of physical disgust as the dark correlative to spiritual illumination. This new edition features an exceptional and completely unexpurgated translation by Alexis Lykiard, and includes complete annotation and an illuminating introduction.

PSYCHOPATHIA SEXUALIS *Krafft-Ebing*

Lustmurder, necrophilia, pederasty, fetishism, bestiality, transvestism and transsexuality, rape and mutilation, sado-masochism, exhibitionism; all these and countless other psychosexual proclivities are detailed in the 238 case histories that make up Richard von Krafft-Ebing's legendary *Psychopathia Sexualis*. Long unavailable, this landmark text in the study of sexual mania and deviation is presented in a new, modern translation highlighting the cases chosen by Krafft-Ebing to appear in the 12th and final edition of the book, the culmination of his life's work compiled shortly before his death.

An essential reference book for those interested in the development of medical and psychiatric diagnosis of sexual derangement, the *Psychopathia Sexualis* will also prove a fascinating document to anyone drawn to the darker side of human sexuality and behaviour.

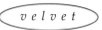
HEAT *Candice Black (editor)*

A compendium of erotic and sex-related photography, art and literature, featuring selections from past, present and future *Velvet* publications as well as material unique to this edition.

Photography: Richard Kern, Araki, Romain Slocombe, Peter Whitehead and Simon Starkwell, plus '70s porno cinema.

Writing: the Marquis de Sade, Terence Sellers, Lydia Lunch, Jeremy Reed, Peter Sotos, Krafft-Ebing and many others.

Graphic art: the complete 50-page version of Romain Slocombe's underground S/M classic *Prisoner Of The Red Army!*.

TORTURE GARDEN *David Wood (Editor)*
From Bodyshocks to Cybersex...A Photographic Archive of the New Flesh

A unique, definitive and breath-taking 5-year photographic record of Torture Garden – described by Marquis magazine as "the world's largest and probably most famous fetish club".
  This deluxe book explores and celebrates the boundaries of the body and human sexuality with an extraordinary collection of images by the scene's two leading photographers, Jeremy Cadaver and Alan Sivroni.
  An extensive collection of literary quotes juxtaposed with these stunning photographs helps create an anthropological, psychological and cultural backdrop to Torture Garden's position at the frontier of the fetish/body art phenomenon. The book includes some 350 original photographs, with over 50 colour plates.

BABY DOLL *Peter Whitehead*

1972 found Rolling Stones documentarist Peter Whitehead ensconced in a chateau in southern France with a teenage heiress model and a month's supply of film and psychedelic drugs. The startling results, never before published, are contained in *Baby Doll*, a beautiful yet disturbing visual diary of a lost four weeks spent in the pursuit of both physical and spiritual erotic extremes.
  An uncensored, unflinching photographic journal of sexual metamorphosis and personality disintegration, *Baby Doll* is also a unique testament to Peter Whitehead's experimental vision, a forbidden legacy of an era simultaneously marked by its innocence and its license to explore previously uncharted areas of sexuality and psychic experimentation.

CITY OF THE BROKEN DOLLS *Romain Slocombe*

Tokyo metropolis. Both in hospital rooms and on the neon streets, beautiful young Japanese girls are photographed in plastercasts and bandages, victims of unknown traumas. These are the "broken dolls" of Romain Slocombe's Tokyo, a city seething with undercurrents of violent fantasy, fetishism and bondage.
  Not since J G Ballard's legendary *Crash* have the erotic possibilities of trauma – real or imagined – been so vividly exposed. *City Of The Broken Dolls* is a provocative, often startling Photographic document of a previously unseen Tokyo, and of the girls whose bodies bear mute witness to the city's futuristic, erotic interface of sex and technology.

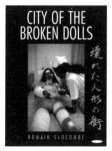

VELVET PUBLICATIONS

INFORMATION

You have just read a *Velvet* book
Published by:
Velvet Publications
83, Clerkenwell Road, London EC1R 5AR
Tel: 0171-430-9878 Fax: 0171-242-5527
E-mail: velvet@pussycat.demon.co.uk

Velvet publications should be available in all proper bookstores; please ask your local retailer to order from:

UK & Europe: Turnaround Distribution, Unit 3 Olympia Trading Estate, Coburg Road, Wood Green, London N22 6TZ
Tel: 0181-829-3000 Fax: 0181-881-5088

Italy: Apeiron Editoria & Distribuzione
Pizza Orazio Moroni 4
00060 Sant'Oresta (Roma)
Tel: 0761-579670
Fax: 0761-579737

USA: Subterranean Company, Box 160, 265 South 5th Street, Monroe, OR 97456
Tel: 541-847-5274 Fax: 541-847-6018

USA Non-booktrade: Xclusiv, 451 50th St, Brooklyn, NY 11220
Tel: 718-439-1271 Fax: 718-439-1272
Last Gasp, 777 Florida St, San Francisco, CA 94110
Tel: 415-824-6636 Fax: 415-824-1836
AK Distribution, PO Box 40682, San Francisco, CA 94140-0682
Tel: 415-864-0892 Fax: 415-864-0893

Canada: Marginal, Unit 102, 277 George Street, N. Peterborough, Ontario K9J 3G9
Tel/Fax: 705-745-2326

Japan: Tuttle-Shokai, 21-13 Seki 1-Chome, Tama-ku, Kawasaki, Kanagawa 214
Tel: 44-833-1924 Fax: 44-833-7559

A full catalogue is available on request.

ORDER FORM

(please photocopy if you do not wish to cut up your book)

TITLE (please tick box)	PRICE	QUANTITY	TITLE (please tick box)	PRICE	QUANTITY
☐ The Lusts Of The Libertines	£7.95		☐ Flesh Unlimited	£7.95	
☐ Dungeon Evidence	£9.95		☐ The Whip Angels	£4.95	
☐ The Velvet Underground	£7.95		☐ House Of Pain	£4.95	
☐ Whiplash Castle	£7.95		☐ Irene's Cunt	£7.95	
☐ The Snake	£7.95		☐ Psychopathia Sexualis	£9.95	
☐ The Black Rose	£7.95		☐ Torture Garden	£16.95	
☐ Philosophy In The Boudoir	£7.95		☐ Baby Doll	£12.95	
☐ The She Devils	£7.95		☐ City Of The Broken Dolls	£12.95	
☐ The Pleasure Château	£7.95		☐ Heat	£14.95	

Total Amount £_____ ☐ I enclose cheque/money order ☐ I wish to pay by ☐ Visa ☐ Mastercard

Card No: |__|__|__|__|__|__|__|__|__|__|__|__|__|__|__|__| Expiry_____

Signature_____Date_____

Name_____

Address_____

_____Telephone_____

Please add 10% to total price for postage & packing in UK (max. £5.00) 20% outside UK (max £10.00).
*Make cheques/money orders payable to **Velvet Publications** and send to 83 Clerkenwell Road, London EC1R 5AR (Sterling only)*